OFFICIAL TROPICO™ STRATEGY GUIDE

BY HOWARD A. JONES

LEGAL STUFF

Brady Publishing
An Imprint of
Pearson Education
201 W. 103rd St.
Indianapolis, IN 46290

ISBN: 0-7440-0078-5

Library of Congress Catalog No.: 2001-135046

Printing Code: The rightmost double-digit number is the year of the book's printing; the rightmost single-digit number is the number of the book's printing. For example, 01-1 shows that the first printing of the book occurred in 2001.

04   03   02   01   4   3   2   1

Manufactured in the United States of America.

BradyGAMES Staff

DIRECTOR OF PUBLISHING
David Waybright

EDITOR-IN-CHIEF
H. Leigh Davis

MARKETING MANAGER
Janet Eshenour

CREATIVE DIRECTOR
Robin Lasek

ASSISTANT LICENSING MANAGER
Mike Degler

ASSISTANT MARKETING MANAGER
Susie Nieman

Credits

TITLE MANAGER
Tim Cox

SCREENSHOT EDITOR
Michael Owen

BOOK DESIGNER
Dan Caparo

PRODUCTION DESIGNERS
Jane Washburne
Bob Klunder
Tracy Wehmeyer

TABLE OF CONTENTS

ACKNOWLEDGEMENTS AND THANKS

This strategy guide wouldn't have been possible without the assistance of those Tropico geniuses, Phil Steinmeyer and Franz Felsl. Thanks for taking the time to answer all those questions so promptly. This is a great game, and I loved playing it—which made writing this book a lot simpler.

A group of play testers provided invaluable information about Tropico strategies, and I am grateful to them all: Scott Vail, Chien Yu, Joe Covello, Frank Kirchner, Stacey Sharpe, Ryan Littlefield, and Lisa Nawrot. Thank you all!

Tim Cox and Ken Schmidt at BradyGAMES helped test strategies and supplied some great suggestions (Ken racked up some impressive scores along the way!). Thanks guys.

Thanks also to Leigh Davis for assigning me this project, and the whole crew at BradyGAMES, who work harder than you know to produce books like this.

Lastly, thanks to Shannon, Darian, and Rhiana, who understood I was working hard even if I was having fun, and who cleared out to make the writing easier. It's great to have you back!

A BIG THANK-YOU FROM BRADYGAMES

Everyone at BradyGAMES would like to extend a heartfelt thanks to all those who helped create this strategy guide. In particular, Aaron Rigby and Jamie Leece of Take 2 Interactive, Phil Steinmeyer and Franz Felsl of PopTop, and Devin Winterbottom of GOD Games. Your support and dedication was very much appreciated!

INTRODUCTION

Welcome to Tropico, el Presidente! I'm sure your rule will be an enlightened and profitable one. The little people are certain to love you, especially if you follow the principals set forth in this handy strategy guide.

Tropico may be a tiny tropical island, but its management is very complex to all but accomplished leaders like you. There are countless factors that you must monitor to keep your economy productive and your people happy—if you are worried about that sort of thing.

This book is organized into the following sections:

▷ **Chapter 1, Starting from Scratch:** This chapter shows you how to generate your very own island and dictator.

▷ **Chapter 2, Managing Your Island:** This chapter provides a wealth of information any wise Presidente needs for managing resources, keeping factions happy, and controlling groups of people.

▷ **Chapter 3, Managing Industry & Tourism:** This chapter gives you thorough information concerning the management of all the industries on your island, from corn farms to canneries and hotels.

▷ **Chapter 4, Managing People:** This chapter provides details about the different kinds of citizens on Tropico. It also supplies information about increasing and decreasing salaries and monitoring individuals.

▷ **Chapter 5, Buildings & Structures:** This chapter is all about the structures in the game, which people work there, and each building's purpose. Lastly, it provides a wealth of useful statistics concerning them all

Chapter 6, Edicts: Throwing Money At the Problem: Don't overlook this chapter. Edicts are a wonderful boost to your regime, regardless of the victory conditions you chose or your play style. This chapter provides information on every edict.

Chapter 7, Victory Strategies: This chapter provides a refresher course on the game interface, lists tips for how to get things up and running, and then provides more specific advice about different victory scenarios. It even has a section for iron-fisted dictators and discusses scoring.

Chapter 8, Pre-Designed Scenarios: This chapter is chock full of information for playing and defeating the pre-designed scenarios in Tropico.

Appendix A, Cheats: This chapter contains information useful to the very desperate dictator. Out of money? People ready to overthrow you and you can't think of any options? Look here if all hope is lost...

Appendix B, Quick Reference: This appendix is a quick reference to every building and structure you can construct on Tropico. Need to know the beauty score for a prison fast? Look here.

Appendix C, Quick Reference: This chapter summarizes the jobs available on Tropico and the education requirement needed by the citizens. Refer to this sectioin as your island begins to expand its industry and population.

After looking over this wealth of information, your Excellency, your success is assured, especially as your leadership is already a thing of legend!

Buenos Suerte!

CHAPTER 1

STARTING FROM SCRATCH

> "It has been said that democracy is the worst form of government except all the others that have been tried."
>
> —Churchill

So you wish to generate your very own Tropico. Excellent, el Presidente! Do remember that the choices you make when you generate your island have a huge impact on the course of your game. Do your best to generate the right island for the right kind of leader so your stay on Tropico will be that much more pleasurable.

The clever junta at PopTop enables you to determine all the important characteristics of both your island and the personality of its glorious leader. All you need do is manipulate some intuitively constructed charts to get what you want.

If you will permit, el supremo, I suggest that you play through the introductory scenario prepared for you, available at the start of the game. Upon finishing it, I further suggest that before you design your own Tropico, you open up one or two of the pre-designed scenarios and look over the beautiful landscaping and road systems a talented leader like yourself can place on his island.

Now it is time to look at Tropico's characteristics, and plot your career path.

THE ISLAND OF YOUR DREAMS

Doubtless, you already know that to play a random map you need only to click on the lovely image of Tropico on the hand-made tapestry. You immediately see an outline of Tropico and six ways to adjust its attributes. To change the default attributes, all you need to do is click the push pin to a different location.

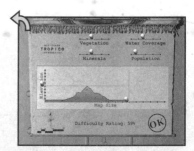

A randomly generated map of Tropico.

▷ **Vegetation:** Vegetation is a reflection of how much foliage there is on Tropico. The more vegetation you have, the easier the time you'll have, especially if you plan on logging. If you plan to bypass logging, you may want to have less vegetation to clear for farms and ranches.

- **Minerals:** The more minerals you begin with, the easier your task will be because you will begin with more natural resources. If you want to try your hand at mining, boost the minerals to their maximum to increase the chance that there will be minerals near your beginning position.

- **Water Coverage:** Water coverage, on the other hand, is the exact opposite. Less water is easier, because then you have more land to farm, mine, live on, and so on.

- **Population:** You can start with between 30 and 70 Tropicans. The number of farms you receive depends upon the population. Starting with more Tropicans lowers the difficulty rating, but it is often easier to keep track of fewer Tropicans, so adjust this as you please.

- **Elevation and Map Size:** These choices determine the island's height and width. Naturally, the lower the elevation and the larger the map, the easier things will be. However, coffee grows best at the highest elevation setting.

Of course, one might be optimistic to use the term "easy" in reference to governing Tropico. Even a low difficulty rating can be a challenge, especially if you have not governed a paradise before. I advise keeping the difficulty in the medium to low range for the first few go-rounds.

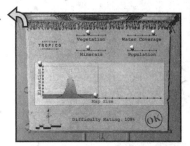

You can end up with some ridiculously difficult situations by manipulating the pushpins.

VICTORY CONDITIONS

Once you've finished generating your island's statistics, you get to select your victory goals. These goals determine your score at the end of the game. They are as follows:

- **A Place In History:** This is one of the most challenging options, for you will score well only if you make your people happy, build your economy, and hide some money away in your Swiss bank account. (Score = Happy Citizens (x2) + Content Citizens (x1) - Unhappy Citizens (x2) + value of Treasury & buildings ÷ 1000 + Swiss account (x5) ÷ 1000)

- **Don't Worry, Be Happy:** Want to try your hand at creating a Utopia? Your victory conditions are not affected by your money, but by how happy your people are. Of course, you'll soon learn that you need money to make them happy, so this is hardly a simple choice either... (Score = Happy Citizens (x4) + Content Citizens (x2) - Unhappy Citizens (x4))

▷ **'Tis Money that Makes the Man:** Who cares about the economy or the whining people, el supremo? Just make as much money as possible. The more you make, the better you'll score. Of course, to make money, you need an economy and you must keep the people from revolting. (Score = Swiss account (x20) ÷ 1000)

▷ **Economic Powerhouse:** Make Tropico the richest island in the Caribbean. With you at the helm, you can turn it into an economic powerhouse. You need not worry about your Swiss bank account unless you desire it, nor your people's happiness, although you'll need them to be at least content for it to work well. (Score = Value of Treasury & buildings (x2) ÷ 1000)

▷ **Open-ended:** This is the victory condition off-switch. Play as long as you want and do what you like, although naturally the Tropicans themselves will have something to say about what you're doing. (No score is determined.)

You select victory conditions, special circumstances, and a few other factors from this screen.

SPECIAL CIRCUMSTANCES

Upon gaining some experience governing Tropico, you might want to make things a little more challenging by changing the circumstances. In order of increasing difficulty, they are:

▷ **A Far Away Place:** Tropico is as far as can be from the U.S., so tourism is less lucrative. You're also less likely to be invaded by the US.

▷ **Rebel Yell:** Tropicans just don't tolerate an el Presidente with vision. As soon as their happiness sours a little, they start running for the woods. Plan on having a healthy military force when choosing this option.

▷ **Free Elections:** When selecting this, the world watches Tropico so closely that you must run fair and honest elections. This means no fraud and no bypassing of elections. Ay Caramba!

▷ **Immigrants Out!** An ugly, anti-immigrant fervor has hit Tropico, and as a result you'll receive no free workforce boosts whatsoever. You can still hire overseas labor for the rough jobs, but you are solely dependent on native Tropicans for labor.

There are three more options you can choose from:

▷ **Political stability:** Your options range from Sandbox mode (disables rebels, uprisings, coups, and elections), which lowers your difficulty level to almost nil, up to the hardest setting called Painful, which can just be ugly. You should probably stick with the lower settings, at least until you get the hang of things. It's not much fun building your first Tropico if you get booted out of office in the first 10 years.

▷ **Economy** also has a Sandbox mode, where you basically have an endless supply of money. Who needs a cheat code? At the other end of the scale is Just Plain Ludicrous, which is just what it sounds like. Try setting the difficulty for not too harsh now, or easy the first times 'round the banana tree.

▷ **Game length** can range from 10 to 70 years. The longer you have to rule, the more time you'll have to boost your score, therefore the difficulty rating is lower on longer games.

Once you're through here, click the OK circle to choose the attributes of your dictator.

DICTATOR ATTRIBUTES

Choosing your background is like picking the ingredients that will go into a rum cake. You must blend them carefully to get what you desire in the end. The right amount of the right things results in a strong, vigorous taste with subtle shadings of other qualities. A poor amount, or too much of one ingredient, and your cake will turn out poorly—although I would never suggest el Presidente was half baked!

Your excellency can either page through the pre-generated dictators and play one as is, or you can pick one that you want and adjust all of their attributes. You should at least examine their attributes, or you may be in for some nasty surprises. If you want to build a tourist's paradise and end up creating a leader whose characteristics double your island's pollution score, you'll be frustrated indeed!

A dossier on the new Presidente sits on the table near the tapestry.

To start molding your glorious Presidente, click on the View/Edit Dossier option. If you want to throw caution to the wind, just click on Begin Regime.

As you select backgrounds, rise to power, qualities, and flaws, you accumulate pluses and minuses. It is good to accumulate bonuses in a single area, but bad to accumulate minuses in a single area. For instance, if your background is farmer with empathy, and your flaws are compulsive liar and short-tempered, you have a whopping -50% approval rating from the intellectuals. They may be a small faction, but that's a huge minus, and it won't go away.

Either take the minuses in areas you don't plan to use (in industry, for example, if you're going to build a paradise), or in foreign relations if you don't plan to socialize. Or you can take a bunch of big bonuses in one category and arrange it so that the minuses only affect them a little bit.

Strongly consider the victory conditions you selected and the type of island you designed before choosing your qualities. For the greater good of Tropico, I have listed the victory conditions for you once more, along with the qualities a successful ruler must have to succeed.

> ▷ **Place in history:** Try to be as balanced as possible. You'll need money with which to build, and should look for bonuses to educate your people. Also, foreign relations bonuses wouldn't hurt either.

> ▷ **Don't worry, be happy:** You can stack the deck a little toward keeping all factions happy. Choose tourist positive skills, because tourism pollutes less and makes it easier to keep everyone happy. To keep the factions pleased, build to suit their needs before they clamor on them, so you must plan on generating income in some fashion.

> ▷ **'Tis money that makes the man:** Plan on strong-arm tactics, so choose options that make the people easier to repress and less expectant of liberty. The less they expect, the less they will grumble when you delay elections.

> ▷ **Economic powerhouse:** Make choices that will boost factory production and industrial output. You have many options here: You can build your fortune on rum (choose Booze Baron), mining (select Miner as a background) or tourism, in which case you should select options that will increase the love of tourists. You can also plan to build many factories and industries, in which case you should broaden your scope.

With all this in mind, and without further fanfare, here are you choices. Viva el Presidente!

TIP

Make sure you check out the section called Managing the Factions in the "Managing Your Island" chapter for additional details.

BACKGROUND

The first choice you must make is background. From where does your Excellency hail? It is good to have your future in mind when you decide your past.

Note that it is possible to pick a background quality that gives you a low score in something, and then cancel that low score with another quality. For instance, a Booze Baron gets a –5% with the religious faction, but if you are elected for family values, you get a +15% with the religious faction, bringing you to a +10 total with the religious faction. This score might be further added to or diminished by your qualities and flaws. Oh, there are many choices, el Presidente!

MOSCOW U.

+10% Communist Faction

+30% Russian Relations

+10% Education (and +10% job skill improvement)

-15% U.S. Relations

This is an excellent choice if you plan to work with the communists, although an obviously poor one if you desire to be on the good side of the U.S.

Note also that it is a good boost to your education. You are likely to get tourists from the US more than any other countries, so this is probably a bad choice if you want a tourist's paradise. Of course, you can cancel out the bad U.S. relations by picking other qualities, but one cannot have everything.

HARVARD U.

+10% Capitalist Faction

+30% U.S. Relations

+20% Education (and +20 job skill improvement)

-15% Russian Relations

This is almost the polar opposite of Moscow U. Take note that the education bonus is higher if you come from Harvard. A good choice if you want to have help from the U.S., get a leg up from the capitalists, and help get skilled workers.

MINER

+10% Communist Faction

+10% Capitalist Faction

+50% Miner Productivity

-20% Environmental Faction

Here's a rarity: A choice that pleases both communists and capitalists. If you want to please these factions, this is a good choice. The +50% Miner Productivity bonus is nice, but remember that your mines may show up on the wrong side of the island. You might not have any mines at all, or none worth very much. If you plan to make mining your forte, you can even the odds beforehand and boost the amount of minerals on Tropico during island generation.

FARMER

+10% Communist Faction

+50% Farmer Productivity

-10% Intellectual Faction

This isn't a bad choice at all. The farms are very useful throughout the game, especially in the beginning. If you choose to be a tobacco and rum magnate, this is a great choice. Be careful of accumulating too many negatives against the eggheads, since they are one of the harder factions to appease with edicts. How many do you think there are on Tropico? Do you expect a coup from them? Pfah!

BIBLICAL SCHOLAR

+10% Religious Faction

+5% Intellectual Faction

+10% Education (and +10% job skill improvement)

-15% Crime Rate

The little people, the mother church is close to their heart, el supremo. This choice will please many and boost the education of your workers, and educated workers mean you don't have to hire off Tropico labor for your factories.

MAN OF THE PEOPLE

+20% Communist Faction

-5% Religious Faction

This option gets you in good with one faction and slightly lowers your rating with another. The communists are likely to be one of the more powerful factions, but it is not an excellent choice, unless you pick other characteristics that boost your ratings with other factions. You could create a dictator beloved by many groups.

BOOZE BARON

+100% Rum Revenue (Rum sells at twice the normal price)

-5% Religious Faction

You'll get no immediate benefit from this choice, but once you build a rum distillery... The hindrance to this is that the Tropicans may not have much land that is good for sugar cane, so this can be somewhat risky.

LEFTIST AUTHOR

+10% Communist Faction

+15% Intellectual Faction

+20% Education (and +20 job skill improvement)

This choice puts you in better stead with two factions, and gives you an education boost. A decent selection, indeed.

FORTUNATE SON

+10% Overall Respect

-10% Intellectual Faction

Avoid racking up too much of a negative impact with the intellectuals, since they are difficult to appease. Tropicans are proud of their native son, and all the rest feel more fondly toward you. A good choice if you plan to walk over your people, your Excellency.

SELF-MADE MAN

+10% Capitalist Faction

+10% U.S. Relations

+15% Factory Worker Productivity

An excellent choice if you want better output from your factories and plan to use U.S. aid.

SILVER SPOON

+25% Capitalist Faction

+10% Tourism Rating

+10% Factory Worker Productivity

+20% Starting Cash

-10% Communist Faction

If you were born into the upper-class, you start with a host of benefits. Of course, the largest faction on the island may be ill disposed toward you, but look at all the boosts this option receives!

GENERALISSIMO

+30% Military Faction

-20% Liberty

+15% Soldier Productivity

Ah, you like things to be orderly? This is a good choice then. Your soldiers will shoot more accurately and the military will love you. The people… what do they know about liberty? It is overrated.

CHIEF OF POLICE

+10% Military Faction

-10% Liberty

-40% Crime Rate

Being a former chief of police is like being a low-caliber generalissimo. The military faction still likes you, and the crime rate throughout the island is very low. Build up those tenements, el Presidente, the criminals will not dare show their faces.

DEVELOPER

+20% Capitalist Faction

-10% Environmentalist Faction

+50% Pollution

-20% Building Cost

The reduced building cost may seem attractive, but keep in mind the effect pollution has on tourists. You can probably handle your people, el Presidente, who sometimes do not like the black smoke and fragrant odors, but the tourists will not come to a polluted Tropico. If you don't need any stinking tourists, polluting the island isn't a problem.

NATURALIST

+15% Intellectual Faction

+25% Environmentalist Faction

-30% Pollution

+10% Building Cost

The environmentalists and intellectuals tend to be smaller factions on Tropico. You must build to prosper, el-Presidente, so the building cost hike is problematic. On the other hand, you can counter that with some banks set to urban development, and if you plan to create a tourist's paradise, a low pollution score can be a big help.

PROFESSOR

+20% Intellectual Faction

+50% Education (and +20 job skill improvement)

It is funny to think of the three Tropican intellectuals as a faction, but that education bonus is not to be laughed at. A viable choice if you plan to build many factories. Think how many more Tropicans can be taught skills if the rate at which they are educated doubles!

POP SINGER

+5% All Factions

+10% U.S. Relations

+10% Tourism Rating

+50% Nightclub Effectiveness

Look at all those bonuses, el Presidente. Please, would you sing your song for the people one more time? This is an excellent choice if you desire to build a tourist haven and remain beloved by the people.

RISE TO POWER

How is it that el Presidente came to this post? These options can raise, lower, or cancel out your background choices, so examine them with care. Make selections that complement each other.

How did el Presidente come to power?

COMMUNIST REBELLION

Very Low Democratic Expectations

+10% Communist Faction

+25% Russian Relations

+10% Farmer Productivity

Naturally, the people do not expect much democracy under your enlightened rule if you are elected by the communists, so they will not be too disappointed should you cancel elections. However, you can expect good relations with the Russians and good farmer productivity.

CAPITALIST REBELLION

Low Democratic Expectations

+25% U.S. Relations

+10% Capitalist Faction

+10% Factory Worker Productivity

A good choice if you're a budding industrialist but don't want to worry too much about the election process. The people won't be expecting much from it.

ELECTED AS SOCIALIST

High Democratic Expectations

+10% Communist Faction

+15% Russian Relations

+20% Liberty

This choice nets you good foreign relations and boosts the people's expectation for liberty. I suppose that would be okay, el Presidente, but perhaps you should consider other options.

ELECTED AS FASCIST

Moderate Democratic Expectations

+15% Military Faction

+20% Liberty

-10% Crime Rate

Perhaps you wish to lead your people to a bright new future, but maintain firm control in the process. The crime rate will be low, but there's that ugly liberty word again...

ELECTED AS CAPITALIST

Very High Democratic Expectations

+5% Capitalist Faction

+15% U.S. Relations

+20% Liberty

+20% Factory Worker Productivity

This choice boosts U.S. relations and excites the capitalists. However, it increases the desire for liberty while also boosting factory output.

ELECTED FOR "FAMILY VALUES"

Very High Democratic Expectations

+15% Religious Faction

+20% Liberty

+10% Tourist Rating

A choice that boosts the rating tourists will give Tropico, and puts you in good with the religious faction. Liberty is not always a bad thing either.

MILITARY COUP

Near Nil Democratic Expectations

+20% Military Faction

-20% Liberty

-20% Crime Rate

-25% Military Building Cost

This is the choice if you plan to run things your way. No pesky elections are expected, and no one will mind if you cancel them. If they do, you can squish them. At least it will be easy to keep the streets safe.

RELIGIOUS APPOINTMENT

Low Democratic Expectations

+15% Religious Faction

-25% Religious Building Cost

It's always nice to get in good with a faction, but let's face it, there are only two religious buildings you can construct, so that -25% isn't as big a deal as it looks. Sure, you might put up a few churches, but still...

INSTALLED BY KGB

Very Low Democratic Expectations

+10% Communist Faction

+40% Russian Relations

-30% Liberty

Uneducated allowed to be
  soldiers

Another good choice if you plan to repress... er, guide, your people. It puts you in good with what's likely to be the largest Tropican faction. It enables anyone to be a soldier in your employ, and lowers expectations for liberty and elections. That doesn't mean people will be happy, mind you.

INSTALLED BY CIA

Low Democratic Expectations

+10% Capitalist Faction

+40% U.S. Relations

-30% Liberty

$2000 Annual CIA Stipend

That extra two grand a year can be especially nice near the start of the game. If you're in it for the money, give this one a try.

BOUGHT THE ELECTION

Low Democratic Expectations

-5% Intellectual Faction

Can commit election fraud with lower consequences

If rigging elections is the only way you can stay in power, this is a great choice. It lets you alter 10% more ballots and raise only half the outrage from the people. They're used to your handiwork.

HEIR APPARENT

Low Democratic Expectations

+10% Overall Respect

Beloved son of a beloved ruler (or perhaps feared, your Excellency?), the people hold great respect for you

POSITIVE TRAITS

As with the other personality traits, choose ones that boost traits in a positive fashion while minimizing any negative traits.

CHARISMATIC

+5% All Factions

+50% Radio/TV Dogma Effectiveness

This gives you a leg up with everyone. If chosen, don't forget to take advantage of the media, for which you need a power plant. If you're worried about getting on the wrong side of the people with your activities, select this trait.

HARDWORKING

+10% Overall Productivity

Everyone will emulate your hardworking traits and do that much more for the good of Tropico.

FINANCIAL GENIUS

+10% Capitalist Faction

+20% Factory Worker Productivity

-25% Bank and Shop Cost

This is an excellent choice for anyone planning to build an industrial wonderland. Look at the productivity bonus and the reduction on banks and shops! Banks, remember, can reduce the cost of buildings, so build plenty using this trait.

GREEN THUMB

+10% Environmentalist Faction

-10% Factory Worker Productivity

-50% Pollution

This wouldn't be a bad choice for some-one wanting a tourist's paradise considering the low pollution score. Note also the low factory productivity, which isn't a big issue if you're planning on a tourist industry.

ADMINISTRATOR

+10% Education (and +20 job skill improvement)

-10% Building Cost

Hmm, if you start with this -10% building cost and then construct some banks and set them for urban development, you could save a lot of money. And look at that bonus for educating and training workers...

DIPLOMAT

+5% U.S. Relations

+5% Russian Relations

Start with Embassy

If you want to play with the big boys, this is a good choice. This gives you better foreign aid right from the start.

EMPATHY

+10% All Factions

-10% Intellectual Faction

It can't hurt to get on the good side of everyone, although you should steer clear of ramping up the negative impact against the intellectuals. They are the most difficult to please when using edicts.

ENTREPRENEURIAL

+10% Foreign Trade

This increases all export prices 10%, which is great if you're building a crop or industrial export-based economy, but not so good for a tourist's paradise.

INCORRUPTIBLE

+10% Religious Faction

+10% Intellectual Faction

-30% Crime Rate

Swiss Bank Prohibited

If you're planning on being generous anyway, choose this option, lower the crime rate, and get in good with a couple of factions in the process.

SCHOLARLY

+20% Intellectual Faction

+30% Education (and +30% job skill improvement)

This is another good choice for boosting your industry.

FLAWS

Unfortunately, not everyone's perfect, although you come much closer than most, el Presidente. How shall we classify those final traits that make you uniquely the Presidente we know and love?

Flaws are tricky. You must try not to pick any that will counteract all of your hard-chosen traits. Not everything about a flaw is bad though—sometimes there are strange benefits.

Oh well... Nobody's perfect!

KLEPTOMANIAC

-10% Capitalist Faction

-10% Religious Faction

-10% Factory Worker Productivity

+100% Souvenir Shop
  Maintenance

Well, the capitalists may not like you very much anyway or those close to the mother church, but it is a bad thing to have to pay twice the cost to maintain souvenir shops. The -10% factory production is a problem if you've been accumulating high bonus points for factory work.

WOMANIZER

-10% Religious Faction

-10% Women's Respect

Remember that the religious faction is apt to be one of the larger factions. Annoying the women means that half the people on the island respect you less, so a religious woman will automatically think 20% less of you than someone else. This won't help you win any popularity contests. On the other hand, this flaw won't interfere quite as overtly with your industrial parks or tourist wonderland.

COMPULSIVE LIAR

-15% Religious Faction

-15% Intellectual Faction

One of the larger factions on the island may like you less, but this choice doesn't interfere with industry or tourism.

UGLY

-5% All Factions

-10% Tourist Rating

Hmm... Everyone likes you a little less, but not that much less. If you are beloved by the people because of some other bonus, you could alleviate this somewhat. Apparently your distinctive looks frighten foreigners, but if you are an industrialist, who cares?

ALCOHOLIC

-15% Religious Faction

-5% Global Productivity

+10% Russian Relations

It's never good to lower productivity, but -5% isn't that bad if you've already raised it elsewhere. Church-goers don't approve of your interest in the fruit of the vine, but the Russians do.

FLATULENCE

-20% U.S. Relations

-10% Russian Relations

Palace Guard Double Salary

Well, there are only four palace guards, so this option isn't too bad if you don't plan much foreign involvement. If you do, avoid this flaw.

COMPULSIVE GAMBLER

-10% Religious Faction

The church and her children do not think highly of your hobby. The other drawback is your yearly binge, which will drain between $300 and $1,500 pesos from the treasury. It's not a large amount, your Excellency, although it might add up in lean years. Also, about 1 out of every 5 years, your Excellency experiences a winning streak, and wins $300 to $1500 instead of losing.

PARANOID

-10% All Factions

+10% Military Faction

Police Resented Like Soldiers

Everyone hates you a little more, except for the fascists. Well, the fascists all have guns, so it's not a bad thing to be on their good side, especially if you wear the velvet glove, el supremo.

COWARD

-5% Military Faction

Soldiers and supporters twice as likely to flee in battle.

This is an awful choice if you plan to repress your people. If you're truly working with the people's best interests at heart and need not fear much rebellion, this is a good choice.

MORONIC

-50% Education (and -50% job skill improvement)

Universities Prohibited

Since every successful regime needs homegrown skilled workers, this is an awful choice. Take careful note of the low job skill improvement. I humbly suggest that you avoid this choice at all costs, although in a pinch you might take it if you desire to only make pesos. However, pay attention to the lowered skill improvement of your workers, who will not get as good at their jobs as fast, and hence make less money.

SHORT TEMPERED

-15% Intellectual Faction

-10% Military Faction

We have had many good jokes about the eggheads, but keep in mind that you do not want to accumulate too many minuses related to them.

POMPOUS

-20% U.S. Relations

+30% Edict Cost

If you don't plan to use many edicts or worry about U.S. relations, this is a good pick. Face it, though, edicts are very useful.

TOURETTE'S SYNDROME

-5% All Factions

-15% U.S. Relations

-15% Russian Relations

$1,000 Pay-Per-View Revenue

Your yearly address is so beloved by the world that they pay to see it. The people think a little less of you (although this low number can be counterbalanced if you have bonuses elsewhere) and foreign relations are bad. But if you don't plan on using the foreigners, and want a little extra cash...

CHEAPSKATE

-10% Communist Faction

-5% Building Cost

Restricted Worker Pay

This isn't a great flaw to pick, since you can't pay your workers more than $25 dollars a month and educated workers won't care for it much. On the other hand, if you never plan to use many of them (do you plan to fill the isle with tobacco plants and sugar cane fields and logging camps?), then you have little need to pay workers much. The slight building cost reduction is an option if you plan to play a shorter game.

RELIGIOUS ZEALOT

+5% Religious Faction

-25% Intellectual Faction

+50% Church Visits

The intellectuals won't like you as well, but church attendance will be up, which means religious satisfaction will be up to. This isn't a bad choice at all, as long as you remember to placate the intellectuals with a high school, or counterbalance this choice with an intellectual bonus somewhere else. If you choose this, build a church early.

GREAT SCHMOOZOLA

-20% Intellectual Faction

-10% U.S. Relations

-10% Russian Relations

+10% Respect of Least
    Intelligent

This flaw will actually increase respect for you amongst a segment of the populace. A bad choice if you're currying favor with the superpowers, but again, not a bad selection.

CHAPTER 2

MANAGING YOUR ISLAND

> "Those who cast the votes decide nothing. Those who count the votes decide everything."
>
> —Stalin

On the whole, managing your island comes down to managing your people and to manage them, you need to monitor how they feel.

When you start the game, everyone is content because they are hopeful about what your leadership will bring to the island. They won't stay content for long though. After 10 years or so, the people grow more restless. Only by improving their happiness can you avoid an uprising. There are 10 factors that determine the happiness of every citizen on Tropico:

- ▷ Food
- ▷ Housing
- ▷ Religion
- ▷ Entertainment
- ▷ Health Care
- ▷ Crime
- ▷ Environment
- ▷ Liberty
- ▷ Job Quality
- ▷ Respect for their Leader

MONITORING THE TEN HAPPINESS FACTORS

Keeping a close eye on the aforementioned factors will go a long way toward keeping your people content. There are a number of ways to monitor these factors.

INFO MODE

By clicking on the big eye button, you enter info mode. Once there, click on the thumbs up button to enter an area where you can learn the overall happiness of your people in any of the 10 aforementioned factors.

Monitoring your people's overall happiness with food quality.

By clicking on each of the icons of these factors (food, housing, and so on), you can see how your people feel about each one. A colored arrow appears over each citizen of Tropico. The greener the arrow, the more pleased they are about the factor.

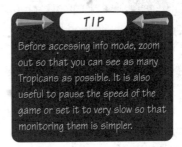

TIP

Before accessing info mode, zoom out so that you can see as many Tropicans as possible. It is also useful to pause the speed of the game or set it to very slow so that monitoring them is simpler.

Obviously, the more factors with green arrows, the more pleased your people will be with your regime. The more red arrows, the closer you are to being overthrown—although that's discussed elsewhere in detail.

You can also click on the people (the icon with three people), and then click on the happiness icon for a good sense of your people's overall well being. The more green arrows you have, the more happy people are overall.

THE ALMANAC

You can also monitor your people's happiness by using the almanac. The almanac appears at the end of every year, but you can access it at any time by pressing the A key.

When the almanac appears, click on the Overview tab. This takes you to a page that enables you to click for further details on such elements as happiness and average worker pay. Clicking on happiness gives you a breakdown on the aforementioned factors and provides a specific number. The lower a number, the more likely it needs to be addressed.

The Happiness sub-page of the almanac.

TIP

You can also access the Happiness page from the People page of the almanac.

The almanac provides another way of checking the overall feeling of your people. When clicking on the lists page, you learn how many of your people are happy (or content or unhappy), as well as how much respect they have for you, amongst many other qualities. The higher the number on the Respect or Happiness page, the better.

MANAGING FOOD

Keeping everyone happy with food is one of the easiest tasks, since food resources are abundant on Tropico. You can build farms to harvest food crops, or build fishing wharves.

Remember to keep an eye on the population (it's the number in the lower-left under the circle number), and build food farms and wharves appropriately. Each fully staffed farm or wharf produces enough food to feed between 30 to 40 people. On average, fishing wharves are the most efficient food producers per worker. Corn farms are also effective, plus corn grows most anywhere.

Marketplaces ensure a smooth and steady supply of food. Although they never make a profit (food is free on Tropico), they serve two important functions. First, marketplaces are compact and can be placed near dense population centers, reducing travel time for people to get food. Second, marketplaces can collect food from multiple farms and therefore tend to have a steadier supply of food. Also, once teamsters haul food to a marketplace, they never haul it away—it waits for the common people to collect it.

Make sure you provide marketplaces for the people.

Building restaurants also affects the quality of food for those who use them, but restaurants are primarily for entertainment.

The social edict Food for the People affects how your people feel about food quality. Note, however, that it doubles food consumption, so you shouldn't use the edict unless you have double the amount of food supply that you need. Issuing it raises the quality of food by 30%.

To review the food quality rating, access the almanac and click on the People tab. One of the numbers there provides an all-around food quality rating. You can click on the words Food Quality to get even more information on meals produced and eaten. Excess food is usually exported for cash.

MANAGING HOUSING

Housing may be only one of 10 factors on Tropico, but it's one of the most important. Your people just don't like living in shacks. When the game begins, your people have enough food, but all they have to live in are shacks. You need to do something about it right away.

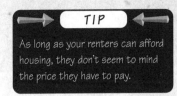

TIP

As long as your renters can afford housing, they don't seem to mind the price they have to pay.

Briefly, to keep your people happy, build some tenements early in the game and apartments in the middle of the game and set them to normal maintenance. Make sure you set the rent to no more than one-third of the combined salary of a married couple.

To provide better housing for your upper class, erect houses or luxury houses and then raise the rent to only what someone in their income class can afford. This varies, naturally, because it all depends upon the salaries of the people. (The "Buildings & Structures" chapter provides specific details about each kind of housing unit you can provide for your people.)

Building an apartment complex.

On occasion, you may need to quickly construct some buildings when the population is angry about the housing situation. This may also occur if you need a place for your construction workers to live while they're working at a remote site. If this situation arises, bunkhouses are your best bet. Just make sure you eventually build something better and tear down the other housing once better accommodations are in place.

How do you stay on top of your housing situation? As with managing your food, keep a constant watch on the population counter in the lower-left of the game screen. However, it can be difficult to remember the number of vacancies. It's better to keep an eye on your most recently constructed apartment. As soon as it's about two-thirds full, build another one even if it stands empty for a while. If you're concerned about your people's housing, it's always good to have a buffer.

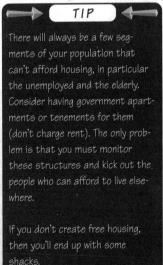

TIP

There will always be a few segments of your population that can't afford housing, in particular the unemployed and the elderly. Consider having government apartments or tenements for them (don't charge rent). The only problem is that you must monitor these structures and kick out the people who can afford to live elsewhere.

If you don't create free housing, then you'll end up with some shacks.

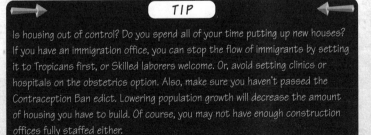

TIP

Is housing out of control? Do you spend all of your time putting up new houses? If you have an immigration office, you can stop the flow of immigrants by setting it to Tropicans first, or Skilled laborers welcome. Or, avoid setting clinics or hospitals on the obstetrics option. Also, make sure you haven't passed the Contraception Ban edict. Lowering population growth will decrease the amount of housing you have to build. Of course, you may not have enough construction offices fully staffed either.

HOUSING QUALITY

All housing has an inherent quality rating, as detailed in the "Buildings & Structures" chapter. However, this rating is modified by other factors.

If a home is in a crime-ridden or polluted area, its quality will be reduced slightly. The worse your home quality, the more the people living there will be unhappy with their housing situation.

To get a good quality rating, place some landscaping around your homes and make sure you have police protection (more details on this in the *Managing Crime* section later in the chapter). Build them upwind of pollution generators like factories.

This house is next to a teamster's office and a bunch of shacks, which lowers its quality rating.

MANAGING RELIGION

Most Tropicans have a need for religion in their lives. The easiest way to provide this is to give them a church early on.

A church, though, requires high school educated workers, and you want it fully staffed. You'll probably build a church before a high school, so plan to pay some extra cash to pay for some priests to come from overseas. Also, only those men religiously inclined can work as priests. Pay those working there well to keep them from leaving.

A fully-staffed church.

Your people's religious scores don't change the instant that you build a church. They need time to get to the church and attend a service before their feelings change about the amout of religion you provide. If you want your Tropicans to have a really high religion score, then build a Cathedral and keep it fully staffed as well.

Keep your cathedral fully staffed.

Build your cathedral on some other part of the island, so that Tropicans don't have to walk far to attend. Plan to pay out some pesos to get it fully staffed (it's even more expensive, as Bishops are college educated).

TIP

Monitor your church and cathedral, because bishops are often elderly and will eventually die or retire. Sometimes priests will leave; try to keep both types of buildings fully staffed.

IMPROVING THE RELIGION SCORE

If your have built the right buildings and given your people time to visit them and your religion score still isn't up, you can consider a couple of measures. Edicts are the easiest way to appease the religious faction. Be careful which edicts you use, though. Bringing in the Pope will work wonders, but you need cordial or better relations with the religious faction, a cathedral, and 10,000 pesos.

If you need to improve relations with the church (say you're working toward getting a Papal Visit), build it up with some smaller edicts. A Contraception Ban will please the religious faction, although at the price of annoying the intellectuals by 30%! It will also increase your population growth. Prohibition will give you a +10% boost, but it increases crime by 100%! An Inquisition lowers liberty scores and tourism, but doubles church attendance, so it is apt to raise religion scores a little.

Because most of these edicts harm other factions more than they help the religious one, it might be best to activate them for just a short time. If you can get relations cordial or better with the religious factor, then bring in the Pope and cancel the other edicts. Lingering good feelings about the Pope's visit will remain.

MANAGING ENTERTAINMENT

Your people crave entertainment and if you don't build any for them, you will be notified that your people are tired of staring at grass.

Consider adding a pub, the cheapest and easiest to build of the entertainment structures. Put it up near a group of housing.

Don't think you're done with entertainment just because you put up a pub! Before you put in a second pub, build a restaurant. It doesn't end there. Throughout the game, you'll need to add new entertainment to increase your people's entertainment score. (The "Buildings & Structures" chapter has more specifics.)

A low quality pub, also known as a dive.

You can raise the quality of an entertainment facility by adding a dress code or upping it to linen tablecloths. The higher the quality, the more pleasing it will be to the people. Keep in mind that if you add a dress code, some segments of society won't be able to attend, in which case you need to have a similar facility for them without a dress code.

ENTERTAINMENT EDICTS

Most of the edicts that improve entertainment also improve tourism. The "Edicts" chapter has complete details, but in summary, the one you'll want to use most, and can use soonest (it only requires a pub), is the Mardi Gras edict. It gives a boost to your people's entertainment score for three years. The Headliner edict and the Pan-Caribbean Games edict also increase the people's entertainment value.

MANAGING HEALTH CARE

Snake oil medicine will only please your people for so long. Eventually they will clamor for health care.

Set your first clinic to preventative medicine, and then hire some overseas labor. Make sure it's fully staffed, and keep the doctors happy by paying them well and providing nearby upscale housing.

Like other college-educated workers, doctors tend to be a little older, so you should monitor their age and replace them the moment they retire.

This gerontology clinic is well staffed.

You can set up a number of clinics throughout the city, but it's better to build hospitals. On an average-sized map, you may need two or three if you want the people to appreciate health care.

TIP

If you construct multiple clinics and hospitals, make sure you spread them throughout Tropico rather than clustering them all in the same spot. It will make accessing them much simpler.

If you want to increase the island's birth rate, set the clinics/hospitals to obstetrics; otherwise, your best benefit is to set them for preventative medicine. If your victory conditions involve population, setting some of the hospitals to gerontology helps keep the aging population alive a little longer, providing they visit the health care facility.

For a good health care system, plan on building a college to educate your own doctors. By doing this, you won't have to import all of them from overseas.

Health care is not a quick-fix situation. If your population is in the red about health care, slapping down a hospital and a clinic won't suddenly improve things. They'll need time to get to the clinics and hospitals to get their health care needs filled.

MANAGING CRIME

Crime management won't be much of a problem for the first fifteen or twenty years. An average-sized map may ultimately require two or three police stations, unless you're building a tourist paradise, in which case you might want one or two more.

Before building a police station, access the info bar and click on the Overall icon (the one that looks like an island). From there, click on the Crime Rate icon. Now zoom out so you can see all of the inhabited areas of Tropico. Areas in green are the most crime free; the redder an area, the more prone to crime it is. Place your police stations in the red area.

You can set a police station to normal training or special ops. Special ops learn 50% faster but like their job 15% less. Consider making them special ops to boost their experience, and then put them back on normal training so they like their job better.

TIP

After building a police station, you can view the crime rate at any time by clicking on the police station itself.

To be fully functional, a police station must be fully staffed, so hire overseas labor if needed. Hopefully, by the time you build the first police station, you'll have a high school and some high school graduates to work there.

MANAGING THE ENVIRONMENT

The environment is one of the 10 qualities that affect your people's feelings toward their ruler. You can check on their overall rating of the environment at any time by clicking the central control panel and clicking on the eye, which takes you to info mode. Once there, click on the thumbs up icon.

Looking at the happiness of people with the environment.

This indicates your people's happiness with the environment, which may be even more important than the condition of the environment itself. Arrows will appear over the heads of the Tropicans on-screen. Zoom out so you can see as many Tropicans as possible. The more orange and red arrows their are, the worse they feel about the environment.

Info mode can provide another measure of the environment. Click on the little island icon, or the "overall" icon. Nine modes are available here, but the environmental option is the one that should interest you. The arrow at the bottom enables you to cycle between overall environment, beauty, and pollution.

Environmental beauty shows where the most beautiful areas on Tropico are located. Ugly buildings (shacks and factories) detract from beauty, while landscaping helps improve it. The greener the area, the more attractive it is.

Coastlines and forests are naturally beautiful.

Environmental pollution shows you the most pollution-free environments, and those that are most polluted. The more red the area, the more polluted it is.

There is one more place to check your overall environmental score. Access the almanac by pressing the A key, and then go to the Politics page and select factions by clicking on the factions hyperlink. This enables you to see what the environmentalists think of your policies.

Look at your environmental faction by accessing the almanac and clicking factions on the Politics page.

POLLUTION

Pollution comes from two sources: people and buildings. Roadways and other heavy-traffic areas also become polluted over time. You can prevent people pollution by passing the Anti-Littering Ordinance edict.

Even if you have no heavy industry, Tropico will have building pollution. Farms, construction offices, and teamster's offices all produce pollution. Individually, their pollution scores are low but their numbers add up.

Of course, it is heavy industry and power plants that generate the largest amount of pollution. If you aren't careful, your island could quickly become a stink pit. Depending upon the victory conditions you selected, it may not be a large concern. It will, though, become a larger and larger concern of your population.

PLANNING AHEAD

To manage pollution requires some planning prior to construction. One of the first things you should always do before building is to zoom out while the game is on slow speed and watch the clouds roll past. Wind systems in Tropico are not complex—this is the way the wind blows all the time. Pollution extends in a cone shape from a building in the direction the wind is blowing. El Presidente, the conclusion you have doubtless reached is that you should build your industries downwind of your palace, if nothing else.

Zoom out to watch the prevailing wind.

Never build your tourist facilities downwind of your power plant or cannery! Likewise, if you want the little people more content with their housing, keep their homes out of the path of the pollution.

If you are very clever, you may even plan an approach such that homes are downwind of smaller polluters like farms and the like, although there is luck involved here. If all the good farm land is upwind, you have little choice but to build your houses downwind.

LIMITING POLLUTION OUTPUT

Planning ahead will only protect you so much. A power plant still generates smog, and a cannery still has a bad odor. Fortunately, there are still a few things you can do.

You can enact an Air Pollution edict, which will cut down on pollution by 50%. Be warned, however, that factory maintenance will climb 20%. If you have a lot of factories, this will add up.

If you don't want a sudden reduction of funds, pass this edict the moment you build your first factory. It will cost more, but you will become accustomed to the cost throughout the game. If you wait to pass it until later, the sudden increase in cost may be more than you can afford.

You can switch your power plant to gas, which lowers its pollution output by half but doubles the maintenance cost. Again, use gas from the outset so that your budget is used to the expense.

Switching your power plant to gas.

Do you have fishing wharves? Then switch all of them to clean waste disposal so nearby beaches don't get polluted.

Industries may have other options that you can purchase or select to cut down on pollution. Check the "Buildings & Structures" chapter for further information.

BEAUTIFYING TROPICO

Cutting down on pollution won't solve all of your environmental woes. The "Buildings & Structures" chapter provides a beauty score for every structure that you can build. A quick glance at this score indicates that most buildings rank in the negative. That's right, almost everything makes your paradise less attractive to the populace. Once all those minuses start adding up, they have a significant impact on the overall environment, and the people's feelings about the environment lower accordingly.

To counteract a low environment score, make use of landscaping. This may be too expensive at the start, but should become more of an option as your industry prospers. Look at a building's beauty score before constructing it, and then refer to the landscaping chart at the end of the "Buildings & Structures" chapter.

This lone statue raises the quality of surrounding houses. Quality would be even higher with some landscaping as well.

Provide enough landscaping to a building so that the shrubs and trees at least cancel the negative beauty score. Because your island is sure to have pollution that will effect the overall environment score, it's better to add enough landscaping to more than counteract the building's negative impact.

As a matter of fact, you should budget landscaping into your building schemes for most victory conditions, especially if you want tourists to flock to Tropico. You have the power to make your island a paradise.

If you have logging camps, set them to selective harvest so that the beauty score of an area isn't affected as severely.

You can also pass an Anti-Littering edict. It has no effect on industrial pollution, but will improve the overall environmental score because each individual Tropican is forbidden to litter on the streets. Unfortunately, this will decrease their liberty by 10%, so check your overall liberty rating before enacting this edict.

Passing the Anti-Litering edict.

MANAGING LIBERTY

Liberty is one of the easier qualities to manage, but one of the more difficult to change. For example, there are no edicts to pass that improve an individual's feeling of liberty, but there are many that you can pass that reduce the Tropicans sense of liberty. One sure way to lower the sense of liberty is to cancel an election or cheat on one.

If you start out the game with a set of qualities that makes the population's expectation of liberty low, then they will be very pleased whenever you have regular elections, and your liberty score will slowly rise. If you start the game with a set of qualities that leads people to expect democracy, it is fairly easy to keep them in the green about liberty—simply have regular elections, mostly fair, and don't impose any repressive edicts.

MANAGING JOB QUALITY

Job quality has a lot to do with pay and conditions on the job. Many industries have upgrades that improve job quality (skylights on the cigar factory, as an example) and others have working conditions that you can alter. For instance, many laborers start work at the default Sweat shop mode. Changing this option to Easy-does-it, while lowering production, improves job satisfaction.

Of course, the best and most important job satisfaction control is your workers' salaries. Specifically, workers want to be paid as much as other workers on other islands. For more details on raising and lowering salaries, refer to the "Managing People" chapter.

MANAGING RESPECT

The respect people feel for you is determined primarily by the relations you have with each faction they belong to. The base respect rating is modified by individual factors like bribes, arrests, or eliminations of family members.

One edict provides a respect boost from all Tropicans: the economic edict called Tax Cut. However, it is muy expensivo, el Presidente!

MANAGING FACTIONS

El Presidente, your people organize themselves in groups. An individual will surely belong to two or more factions.

To look at the factions on Tropico, access the almanac and click the Politics page. Click the View Factions option above the graph to see how you're getting along with each faction. On a scale from bad to good, they are Cold, Cool, Fair, Cordial, and Close. To get a look at what the faction is concerned about and to learn who the faction leader is, click on the faction for more detail.

Looking over your relations with the factions on Tropico.

Each faction has its pet interests and to please the faction, your Excellency must take care of their favorite things. They are:

> **Militarists:** Desire an armory, soldiers, and good pay.

> **Religious:** Desire enough churches or cathedrals for the population, but may need a few edicts (especially a visit from the Pope) to improve relations.

> **Capitalists:** Crave a thriving economy with higher industry or tourism. Strive to have their entertainment needs met.

> **Communists:** Want employment, housing, and relatively equal income.

> **Intellectuals:** Most concerned with liberty and education. If these needs are met, the intellectuals are likely to be pleased.

> **Environmentalists:** Require a beautiful Tropico with little pollution.

The characteristics you select when creating your dictator affect how the factions feel toward you throughout the game. If you want to stay on the good side of factions, it is good to choose bonuses when creating your dictator that put you in good with the religious, intellectual, and environmental factions. Those three factions are the most difficult to manipulate in terms of how you run the island.

Communists are easy enough to please as long as housing is taken care of and there are jobs for everyone, while militarists are single focused on having good pay and a general or three for their armory. Capitalists are always the smallest faction, but will love you if you bring industry and entertainment to the isle.

BRIBERY AND INTIMIDATION

There is a final option that involves factions: You can grease the palm of their leader. Yes, el Presidente, money talks! To find the leader of a faction, access the almanac by pressing the A key and then go to the Factions page and select the faction. Click on the picture of their leader until the person appears in the circle window on-screen, then zoom in on them (pausing the game simplifies this process immensely).

Now choose the Bribe edict (costs $1000) and click on the leader. You will improve your standing with the faction leader, her family, and her faction as a result (although not always!). Be warned that the bribe has a lessening effect over the next three years.

You can bribe a faction leader and possibly improve relations between the faction and your regime.

If bribery seems unlikely to work (the faction leader hates you) and they lead an important faction, you could always use the Eliminate edict on them and attempt to bribe their successor. This sort of action is always risky and might result in an even more hostile faction leader.

MANAGING FOREIGN POLICY

While it is perfectly easy to play a game without U.S. or Russian involvement, either superpower can be very helpful to your ambitions. When dealing with either one, you must have a staffed diplomatic ministry. The more experienced the staff (and if the ministry is fully staffed, so much the better), the more impact your foreign policy has upon how either of the superpowers views Tropico.

When dealing with the superpowers, consider taking the diplomat advantage when you create your dictator's skills, so that you start with a ministry. Lastly, familiarize yourself with all of the foreign policy edicts.

Both the U.S. and the Russians can provide developmental aid. Stay on good terms with both of them at first, so that you can receive tenements and apartments at half the cost from the Russians, while getting an electric power plant for half cost and airport plans from the U.S. If you build an airport, you can even send off a trade delegation, which will provide free buildings, take your goods at increased cost, provide skilled workers, money, and many other things.

Getting developmental aid from the Russians gets you tenements and apartments at half cost.

Your first impulse might be to heavily weigh your dictator attributes toward one superpower or another. Instead, choose attributes that will provide bonuses toward both countries, without selecting attributes that give a bonus to one and a minus toward another.

For example, suppose you choose Harvard U. or Moscow U. By doing so, you receive a bonus with one power and a minus with another. Instead, you could choose self-made man or pop singer, which would give you a +10 on U.S. relations. Then for rise to power, you could pick elected as socialist, boosting your Russian relations 15% without impacting your U.S. relations. The trick is to select flaws that don't decrease relations with either (alcoholic will actually boost you with the Russians a little). Unfortunately, you can't issue foreign policy edicts more than once every two years.

IMPROVING RELATIONS

Suppose you've been on the good side of one superpower and want to work with the other. To switch your ministry to the side with which you want to work, issue the Praise U.S. or Russia edict. This should get relations on better footing. Once they are, you can start requesting aid.

ALLIANCE

Feel free to ally with one of the superpowers, because it gets you some free cash each year. Upon establishing an alliance, the superpower you've allied with pays closer attention to your affairs and is more likely to intervene if they become displeased.

INVASION

If you annoy a superpower with which you've been working, they will invade Tropico, thus bringing your rule to a sudden end. Fortunately, it is somewhat difficult to get them to invade unless you boost the political difficulty to painful.

In fact, Russia will never invade unless you ally with them first and then displease them. The U.S. may invade even if they don't have a base on your island; however, this is somewhat rare.

MANAGING ELECTIONS

From time to time, your people will call for elections, el Presidente. If things are going well, they may not call for them as often. If the people are unhappy, though, they may occur more frequently.

As an election approaches, take a moment to see where you stand with the people. A wise Presidente always keeps his finger on the pulse of the people by monitoring the 10 factors discussed previously in this chapter. You can also check on how well you are supported by accessing the almanac. Click on the Lists tab in the almanac and click on Candidate Support. (For this to appear, there must be an upcoming election.)

A quick check of the Candidate Support page will help you decide your strategy.

If you have a lot of people who support you or strongly support you, there won't be much to worry about. Go ahead and hold fair and honest elections.

CANCELING ELECTIONS

When the people call for elections, you are presented with two options. You can either hold elections or cancel them. Canceling them will be less poorly received if the people have low democratic expectations (this depends mostly on how you rose to power). If they have high democratic expectations, the people will be more upset.

Whenever you cancel an election, it lowers your overall liberty rating. When that factor gets too low (as with any of the 10 factors that your islanders care about), things get messy.

Do not cancel two elections in a row, or the chance for unrest and rebellion rises dramatically.

CHEATING

Instead of canceling elections, you can cheat or choose to have the votes counted fairly. During the election year, you must keep a close watch on your support. Cheating causes some resentment (although not nearly as much as canceling an election), so don't use this option too often.

IMPROVING THE VOTE WITH EDICTS

There are other ways to cheat besides counting the votes of dogs and dead men, your Excellency. You can improve the people's mood. Consider using the Mardi Gras edict to improve the people's outlook—a happy Tropican will remember who brought them their happiness.

There are other edicts that boost the entertainment quality of the island, such as the Headliner and Pan-Caribbean Games edicts. You might invite the Pope to drop by (for which you need a cathedral and $10,000), which will definitely gain you favor, although it is a one-time option.

If you have more than enough food, consider passing the Food for the People edict. If pollution is a problem, you can always pass the Air Pollution Standards edict. Is respect a problem? Consider a tax cut; it's like one big bribe to the entire population of Tropico. If you have food reserves, issue the Food for the People edict before an election and cancel it later.

Passing the Food for the People edict raises food quality, but doubles food consumption.

Do you have edicts in effect which displease the people? Consider temporarily lifting some of them (Inquisition, say, or Martial Law).

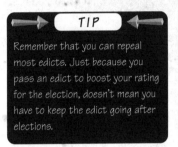

TIP

Remember that you can repeal most edicts. Just because you pass an edict to boost your rating for the election, doesn't mean you have to keep the edict going after elections.

Then, of course, there's always bribery. Bribing your opponent might not work, but a quick check of how well your factions support you can show how certain factions feel. If any factions feel fair or cordial, you can bribe their leaders. This might boost your rating with the whole faction by one level, raising fair to cordial and cordial to close.

TIP

You can always stack the deck. If it's been three years since the last election and things are going well, but you know they might not go so well soon because of plans you intend to implement, consider holding an early election, by using the Early Election edict.

You might even consider putting a hit on the leader of the opposition, although this seldom improves the situation. Instead, it usually angers the opposition even more.

Putting a hit on your opponent.

IMPROVING QUALITY OF LIFE

In addition (or instead of) passing a slew of edicts, you can look over the 10 factors that Tropicans are concerned about, see how you rate in each one, and consider improving your score.

If you're low in the food, housing, or crime category it's difficult to build anything fast enough to alter the course of an election. If you have unoccupied apartments, lower the rent to allow poorer people in. Cut fees at pubs and restaurants to ensure everyone can use them.

Perhaps the easiest way to quickly boost happiness is to increase pay across the board. Keep in mind, though, that pay increases do not immediately improve happiness; it takes about 6 to 12 months. Therefore, raise pay right after an election is declared, and keep wages high until the election ends.

Remember that many industries are set to Sweat shops, so moving them to Easy-does-it is also a simple way to improve job quality. (Remember that construction offices and teamsters can also be set for both options.) After elections, you can always move the settings back to Sweat shop.

REBELS AND UPRISINGS

If you have not played to please all of the people's factors (especially happiness!) or have chosen certain conditions when you generated Tropico (rebel yell, for instance), you will face rebels. When you receive the first message that someone's gone rebel—and you will be dutifully informed when this occurs—it's time to build guard towers.

Construct them on the edges of your civilization. You're unlikely to need more than four, as long as they're fully staffed.

YOUR SOLDIERS

Build homes for the soldiers close to their guard posts, and increase their pay to improve their job satisfaction. This is especially important if you have a lot of rebels, because you'll want to change your soldiers' training to special ops, which means they'll get better twice as fast. On the down side, the soldiers will be less happy about their jobs because of the rigorous training. Take special note that to keep your soldiers happy you can build cabarets, which soldiers especially like.

Only one soldier is employed in this palace— a bad move if you're expecting trouble from the rebels.

EDICTS

No edicts (with the exception of Amnesty) actually reduce the number of rebels, but some edicts reduce the chance of uprisings (Martial Law and Inquisition). Of course, in both cases the cure may be worse than the disease. Issuing such edicts may actually increase the unhappiness of the people and create even more rebels!

To issue an amnesty for the rebels, general conditions (i.e., average happiness) on Tropico must improve by at least 5% since the rebels fled into the woods, or you won't have any rebels interested in rejoining society.

WARNING

It's important to note that the more guard posts you have, the more armories you need. The more armories you have, the more generals you have. The more generals… the more likely you might face a coup.

CHAPTER 3

MANAGING INDUSTRY & TOURISM

"And a woman is only a woman, but a good cigar is a smoke."

—Kipling

Farms, mines, ranches, wharves, and logging camps are industries in their own way, just as much as a smog-belching cannery. This chapter serves as a guide toward running all the industries you can build on Tropico, including what may be the most lucrative and most challenging, tourism.

FARMS, MINES, WHARVES, LOGGING CAMPS, AND RANCHES

These industries are crucial to your survival. Each game begins with a few farms, which you need more of to feed your people. It may also be that Tropico is mineral rich, and a wise Presidente exploits this wealth with mines.

Before you build any of these structures, click on the Info icon (the big eye) and click on the Island icon in the upper-left to get an overall view of the attributes on your island. Three areas should concern you. The first is Overall Crop condition. Clicking here shows you where on the island crops will best grow. The arrow at the bottom of the icon enables you to cycle through all available crops to see where each will best grow. It also enables you to see where cattle or goats will best thrive. As usual, the greener the area, the better suited it is for the activity.

Inspect your overall crop conditions.

You should always check the overall minerals on your island. Suppose you build a slew of buildings only to learn later that they're on a huge gold deposit.

Whoops! Some of those buildings were built right over a huge mineral deposit.

The arrow on the bottom enables you to cycle through the minerals available on your island. The greener an area, the richer it is in resources. However, this can be misleading, because sometimes a small area can contain a lot of wealth.

Lastly, clicking on the Fish icon shows you where the best areas to fish are located. The deeper the better, naturally, which is why wharves are long.

Wondering where best to build you logging camp? El Presidente, build them where there are trees.

MANAGING FARMS, RANCHES, AND FISHING WHARVES

This may well be the easiest task in the game, assuming that you built where the conditions are right for your industry. Leave all the employee slots open if you're producing a cash crop (coffee, sugar, or tobacco). Assuming that you're paying fair or better wages, the slots will soon fill.

Place homes for your workers close to the job site, but don't put them in the best fields or pasture land! The closer the homes are to work, the more time they can spend working rather than traveling.

Marking trees for demolition.

Don't build your farms or ranches in the woods unless you send the construction workers to tear down the trees first. Mark the nearby trees with a bulldozer. Having trees in your field severely cramps the efficiency of a farm, as any farmer will tell you. Farmers can remove trees themselves, if they run out of tasks, but laborers are more efficient.

It takes about two to five years for one of these crops to mature properly, so a wise Presidente will plan ahead and put in the right kind of farms to feed the population or supply factories years ahead of the actual need.

FOOD CROPS

Tropico must supply food to all of its people. Starving people are very likely to revolt, your Excellency, and production is affected as well.

Depending on the skill of its farmers and the quality of land, a farm, ranch, or wharf can produce enough food for between 30 to 40 people, providing that it is fully staffed. (Wharves generally produce more food than the others.)

Some quick math should tell you that 100 people require between three and four farms. To manage your food, always stay a little ahead of the numbers. Grow food crops that are also good for exporting. For example, you can use Pineapples and Bananas as a food source or an export. Fish are also a good export value, but only if canned at a cannery.

You can save a little money by clicking on the blank worker slots before they fill so as to eliminate the number of farmers at one location. If you quickly need more food (if you haven't been watching your population meter often enough), then quickly open these positions by clicking on them. You can fill them even more swiftly by raising the salary. It takes food crops 1.5 to 2 years to grow. Corn is the fastest grower, as a full crop can grow in just over a year.

Fill the blank slots with Xs.

RANCHES

Generally, cattle and goat ranches take longer to get started, since you must build a herd first. If there's some open land, start a ranch or two away from the population center. A small herd needs one farmer; as it grows, hire another one. After about five years, you can start to cull some animals. If you want to export beef, build a smokehouse. In general, use cattle for export and goats for food.

In general, cows need better land and tend to overgraze the land around a ranch much quicker than goats. Cattle ranches are best with lots of land, relatively tree-free.

FISHING WHARVES

Fish, naturally, don't need to be planted, are a steady food source, and may be canned for better export value. Like farms, you don't have to keep them fully staffed unless you're suddenly very short on food. If pollution is a concern, make sure you set the fishing wharves for clean waste disposal when they're built. Fishing is an efficient method of boosting food production, especially if land is scarce.

MANAGING LOGGING CAMPS

Logging has more in common with the heavy industries than it does with farming or ranching. You can upgrade logging camps, plus they employ up to eight workers.

How you manage your logging camp and whether or not you have any at all, depends upon your victory conditions. Logging destroys Tropico's natural beauty. This can be somewhat eased by choosing the selective harvest option, which decreases production rate because your loggers must go further afield for their trees.

A logging camp with a toolshop upgrade.

If you are concerned about the natural beauty of your island or want to make logging a continual staple of your industry, consider the horticulture station upgrade, which allows areas that are cut down to generate at twice the normal speed. The toolshop upgrade decreases cutting time per tree by a whopping 40% and should be considered a wise investment from the start.

As with all industry, you will incur a loss at first until workers start arriving and the first logs arrive at docks for export. Once you have more experienced workers, they will work faster. (**Remember**: You can monitor a worker's experience by clicking on an individual and then clicking on the mortarboard icon to display their skills.)

Logging camps are often in remote locations. Make sure you build housing near the camp as well.

MANAGING MINES

When you select a type of mine, you automatically see the type of mineral that can be mined. Here are two important tips: Make sure you have a specialty mine selected, rather than the "mine all minerals" type of mine, unless you are near several deposits, which is unlikely. In addition, place the mine just outside the area to mine, not directly over the greenest area! Your miners can't pick ax through the bottom of their shacks.

One vein can often support several mines; if it's large enough, you can even construct three or four mines. Different types of mines come with different caveats.

A mine with all upgrades. It is still running at a loss.

> **Iron Mines:** Iron isn't as profitable as the other types. Iron mines are also big polluters and can cause terrain deformations, which are troublesome for building.

> **Bauxite Mines:** These are more profitable than iron mines, but also cause terrain deformation problems.

> **Gold Mines:** Well, your Excellency, if you should be so fortunate as to find a gold mine, then have at it, wherever it may be. When a gold mine becomes productive, consider constructing a jewelry factory to maximize profits.

UPGRADES

All mining upgrades require electricity, and some are only good for certain types of minerals, so read the fine print before you spend money on an upgrade.

Allow me to suggest that you *not* purchase an electrical power plant to power your upgrades unless your mine is already turning a nice profit. If you already have an electrical power plant in place, then by all means, purchase the upgrade!

MANAGING INDUSTRY

No industry on Tropico can make something from nothing. Carefully consider the industrial building you want to erect before spending the money for it. A cannery requires pineapple, coffee, or fish. There is no point in a jewelry factory if you do not have a gold mine producing gold!

Each industry has options that can improve their output, but they have several things in common. Each is built on a simpler industry (a cigar plant requires tobacco, a lumber mill requires logging camps, etc.). Industries typically lose money at start-up. You must often hire inexperienced and inefficient workers, at which point they must build an inventory of raw materials to process. Factories do not post revenues until the goods have been loaded onto a freighter. Don't be alarmed if a factory posts losses over a 10-year period; over time they can be the most lucrative ventures on the island.

A well-manned cigar factory can turn a hefty profit over the years.

Just because you have one farm up and running doesn't mean that it's time to put up a factory. So if you have one logging camp, don't immediately build a lumber mill. One factory can handle the output of three to four farms (or wharves, or mines—whatever simpler industry supplies the raw materials for the factory), and is likely to run into the red unless it has at least two of the smaller industries feeding it with material.

Canneries deserve special attention. If you plan to be an industry magnate, you should always build canneries because they aren't dependent upon just one industry. Pineapples, coffee, and fish may all be canned and sent overseas for profit. Unlike other industries, a single cannery can take in goods from five to six farms!

Of course, el Presidente is certainly aware that factory workers require a high school education, and that Tropico does not have a high school at present. Foreign labor is expensive, and if you intend on building an economic powerhouse, hiring every single high school worker from overseas will become very expensive very fast.

Getting an electrical power plant in place after your factories start turning a profit is extremely important, because many factory upgrades require electricity. Of course, electricity is more useful for some industries than for others.

Get that power plant up and running so your factories can turn more profit.

TIP

To improve job satisfaction by 25%, switch a factory's output from Sweat Shop to Easy Does It. Less work will get done, though.

El Presidente, remember that a worker who likes his or her job better and who is content or happy will work harder for you (although not enough to offset some choices, such as Sweat shop versus Easy Does It). Also, remember that workers who do not have to walk far for their food will spend less travel time between work and home, so consider putting a marketplace between job and home (just because you have one marketplace already doesn't mean you can't have more).

INDUSTRY, INFRASTRUCTURE, AND GOVERNMENT

Roads will make it far simpler for people to reach work quickly, thus enabling your workers to have homes farther away from ugly industrial areas. Roads will also enable them to climb slopes to reach their jobs, and they will likewise improve the speed at which teamsters pick up your goods and take them to the docks.

Keep a close watch on the number of teamsters. Teamsters haul all of your goods to your factories, and then away from your factories to the docks. You typically need one fully staffed teamster office per every four to six farms.

Monitor the number of teamster offices— one per every four farms is more than enough.

That being said, because of the way teamsters work, you must be careful where you place your factories. If your tobacco farm is much closer to the docks than your cigar factory, the teamsters may be inclined to haul it there rather than the factory. Place factories closer to the dock than the industry that supplies the factory, although, as always, you must be mindful of pollution. Consider putting your teamster offices closer to your factories or farms so they don't have as far to go.

The same goes for dock workers, although as mentioned in the "Buildings & Structures" chapter, two docks beside each other isn't as important as providing two means of access. If you've built far from the current dock and goods are piling up for more than three years, then build a new dock so your money can get to you faster. You may also need a new dock when you begin to see your docks with producing sustained output stores of 30 or more. Two docks are usually enough to keep a good-sized industry going, but you may need three if the population is above 500 and geared toward industry.

Crime rates are higher in industrial areas, and a police station near one will go a long way toward improving the people's opinion of the job you're doing keeping the streets safe. This is something you should keep in mind when building housing for your factory workers. As mentioned, they need a high school education, which means that they require better pay. So that they can reach work quickly, you should construct homes near their work places. However, don't build them too close, because areas near industry attract crime, and as mentioned many times already, industry creates pollution.

UPGRADES

Each factory has upgrades. Some are more useful for different factory conditions, while many others require an electrical power plant. Which upgrades you're considering depend upon the victory conditions in your scenario.

LUMBER MILL

▷ **Sawdust Burner:** Cuts the lumber mill's pollution in half, but nothing more.

▷ **Power Saw:** Improves worker production by 30%, and if money is your goal, this is the first upgrade to choose.

▷ **Log Debarker:** Increases worker production 25%, but also requires 10% more logs, so it clears your forests even faster.

CIGAR FACTORY

▷ **Skylights:** Improve worker satisfaction by 15%. A fine thing if the happiness of the people concerns you, but a waste of money otherwise.

▷ **Climate Control:** Enables you to make more cigars, because less tobacco is required for each one.

▷ **Auto-Roller:** Lowers the sales price of each cigar by 10%. On the other hand, an auto-roller increases output by 50%. This is best if you have a lot of tobacco farms and only one cigar factory.

JEWELRY FACTORY

▷ **Skylights:** Improve worker satisfaction with their job by 15%, so it's a good investment if you want to keep the people happy.

▷ **Jeweler's Guild:** Doubles the rate at which your jewelers gain experience. This is a smart investment up front, but not at the end of your rule, as the experience boost will take too long to have an impact.

▷ **Finishing Shop:** Provides a 15% jewelry price boost. If you have a lot of jewelry coming out of your shop and are making a profit, then this is a good investment.

CANNERY

▷ **Packing House:** Provides a 15% production bonus. If you have a cannery, get a packing house for it before your workers start turning a profit.

▷ **Flash Freezer:** Only useful for coffee, nothing else. If you are a coffee powerhouse, this is a must-have from the start, because it ups product value by 25%.

RUM DISTILLERY

▷ **Flavoring Facility:** Increases the value of each barrel 15%. Upon producing a significant amount of rum, add the flavoring facility so you can produce Captain Tropico's spiced rum.

▷ **Mulching Machinery:** Improves worker production by 20%. If you're currently producing a lot of rum and have electricity, this is a smart investment.

EDICTS FOR INDUSTRY

While there are numerous economic edicts, only one is directly useful to your factories, and that is the Industry Ad Campaign. Good for three years, this edict raises the price on all exported goods by 20%. It also requires a television station. If industrial exports are high, build a TV station purely for the purpose of issuing this edict every few years.

Passing the air pollution standards edict.

Another edict can sometimes be useful, but it requires an airport, a diplomatic ministry, and good relations with one of the superpowers. The trade delegation to either U.S or Russia provides aid, but may not succeed unless relations are already good. The resulting aid, however, is randomly generated. Sometimes you receive a boost in export prices, while other times you get a free building (and perhaps not even one you want). You may receive some cash or even free skilled workers. For $1000, if relations are good, you're more likely than not to get something you can use.

Since your industry will soon require an electrical power plant (or possibly even two), consider spending $2000 for a U.S. Developmental Aid edict. Relations with them need to be cool or better. The yanqui dogs will give you plans that cut the construction rate in half for both electrical plants and airports, although you're unlikely to need an airport for anything other than tourism.

TOURISM

So you wish to build a tourist's paradise and bring in the foreign money? Bueno, el Presidente! For that, though, you need beauty, low pollution, and attractions for the tourists to visit. Tourists will free if there's a coup, so if the political terrain is unstable, avoid a tourist's paradise.

Before you build any hotels, access the Info icon (the big eye) and then click on the Island icon to get an overall view of Tropico's characteristics. The arrow on the environmental icon lets you cycle through environmental conditions: you can see where Tropico pollution is and where Tropico is most beautiful. The least pollution and the loveliest plots are green. Don't forget to take note of overall crime. Again, the greener the area, the more crime free it is.

All tourists want a number of things, and if you don't have them, you won't have many tourists. Their wants are:

▷ Attractions and entertainment

▷ Low pollution

▷ Beautiful scenery (including nearby beaches)

▷ Low crime

Low pollution and beautiful scenery are pretty self explanatory, so refer to the section on Managing the Environment in the "Managing the Island" chapter for further details.

Low crime is a different matter. You need one fully staffed police station for every four hotels. Place your police stations close to the hotels.

TOURISM CLASSES

There are three classes of tourism: low, middle, and high. The three main types of hotel (cheap, normal, and luxury) appeal to the tourism classes, and their attractiveness is based on the appropriate rating of their location. Each class craves different types of attractions. The better you please your tourists, the better they will rate the time they have on your island, the more word will spread, and the more tourists will flock to spend their money in Tropico. The types of tourists follow:

▷ **Low-class tourist:** All this type wants is a cheap hotel, a beach, and a pub. They're more forgiving if Tropico has some faults. Rely on this type of tourist if you want some tourism but don't want to make it Tropico's mainstay.

▷ **Middle-class tourist:** This type requires a Hotel (or bungalows, which are much cheaper!), a pub, a restaurant, a beach, and a pool.

▷ **High-class tourist:** Of course, this type requires luxury hotels, all the previously mentioned entertainment, and more! Nightclubs, casinos, sports complexes, the works. The more of these attractions you have, the better (variety, not quantity—no one needs three casinos).

BUILDING WITH THE TOURIST IN MIND

The real money is with the middle- and high-class tourists. Build a pool by each hotel, and place the middle-class hotels fairly close together. Construct the luxury hotels a little further apart from the middle-class hotels and landscape around them.

An upper-class female tourist, yearning for sunny Tropico beaches.

Use the island's attractions as buffers between the rest of the island and the hotels themselves. Pools and spas increase the tourism value of the surrounding land.

TIP

Tourists don't like walking anymore than Tropicans do (perhaps less). Build tourist attractions near their hotels.

To make tourism your main industry, build an electrical plant early (and plan on building more) so that you can build luxury hotels—the sooner, the better. It takes a long time to build an airport, so don't build one unless you plan to rule for a long time (over 50 years). When building an airport, make sure you have plenty of laborers. An airport attracts the wealthier tourists.

Also, consider building a port near the hotels and setting it so that it only receives yachts. You don't need to fully staff a yacht port; ships will dock there as long as there is one person present. You may want to change the setting for docks used by industries to Freighters only. Having yachts and freighters at the same dock lessens the efficiency of tourism and exporting.

TIP

Don't be afraid to raise the attraction rate for tourist attractions. Just make sure you monitor the tourists and see what their max spending level is. Mix up prices so that some attractions are at a higher price for the elite tourist, while others remain low.

Once you start adding attractions, entertainment, and luxury hotels you are likely to need a second electrical power plant. You might also need electrical sub stations to get power to remote but beautiful locations.

Do not forget, el Presidente, that the workers need housing close to the hotels and attractions. Furnish them with apartments or houses so that they do not erect shacks! (If they do so, bulldoze them quickly and supply housing.)

It is possible to maintain your tourist industry without hiring too many overseas workers, although the upscale entertainment and attractions require high school and college educated employees.

TOURISTS AND BANKS

You must not neglect your banking industry if you build up tourism on Tropico. If you set your banks to Tourist's Off-Shore Banking, then the tourists will make money for you in your banks! Impressivo, yes?

Avoid building banks when you get your first cheap hotel and bungalow. Off-shore banking isn't effective until you have hotels or luxury hotels. Also, the more bankers you have on staff, the more accounts you can handle. Build a bank or two in a location where you expect to build tourism later. Set them to Urban Development to receive reduced construction costs. Later in the game as construction slows, and after tourists arrive, switch the banks to Off-Shore Banking to increase profits.

MONITORING YOUR TOURISTS

Want to know what the tourists think of Tropico? There are two ways to monitor their reactions.

Click on any tourist to see their likes and dislikes and how they rate Tropico's tourist industry.

You can click on any tourist walking through the streets of Tropico, or click on any hotel and click on any tourist guest. Upon doing so, you can look at their wants, needs, see what attraction(s) they've visited, and see what their overall tourism rating of the island is.

It would take a long time to look at every tourist's feelings. You can look at all of them by accessing the almanac. Click the Lists tab and select Tourism Rating to see what rating the tourists are giving your beloved Tropico.

The tourists aren't that thrilled with the situation on this Tropico. That's probably because crime is high around all the hotels.

The Lists page of the almanac also enables you to see the country from which most of your tourists come.

Clicking on the Economy tab of the almanac enables you to see how much your tourism is pulling in each year. You can also check for more information on the tourist industry itself.

The Tourism page of the almanac, accessed from the Economics page.

> **TIP**
>
> Don't forget: If you have mostly upper-class tourists, set the buildings and attractions so that they are more upscale, meaning dress codes for the swimming pools, linen cloths at the gourmet restaurants, and so on.

TOURISM EDICTS

A number of edicts directly affect your tourism industry, both positively and negatively. Any edict that a yanqui might consider repressive (such as inquisition or martial law) lowers the rate of tourism. Tread lightly upon the backs of your people if you want the yanqui dollar. You should also avoid the prohibition edict, as it will raise the crime rate by 100%—a definite tourism turnoff.

There are many more edicts that help tourism: a Tourism Ad Campaign (which requires only a hotel and a TV station), The Headliner, which brings in a famous entertainer to a Tropico night-club, hosting the Pan-Caribbean Games, and throwing a Mardi Gras will all boost tourism. Strategically, it is probably best to stagger these events instead of doing them all at once, since many of the edicts are one-time only. You can issue these edicts shortly before elections to boost tourism, fill your coffers, and increase happiness. See the "Edicts" chapter for more information.

CHAPTER 4
MANAGING PEOPLE

"One should guard against believing the great masses to be more stupid than they actually are."

—Hitler

Guiding the little people is no easy task, and someone of your wisdom should take the time to know them a little better. You can divide your citizens into two broad categories: those who work for you and those who do not. But then there are more useful ways to divide them. Economically, your workers fall into three classes: uneducated, high school educated, and college educated. You are unlikely to have very many of the last two when you start the game, but you will need the educated if you are to lead Tropico to its glorious destiny.

The happier your people are, the more work they will do for you, and the more money they will make. Unfortunately, it costs money to make the people happy. It is quite a dilemma, el Presidente.

MONITORING THE MASSES

While it is useful to monitor some individuals closely, particularly the college educated and your loyal soldiers (we must ensure that they are loyal, eh, el Presidente?), it is often more useful to test the mood of your people by referring to the almanac. It automatically pops up at the end of the year, but you can see it at any time by pressing the A key.

The People page of the almanac shows an overview of numerous things. It lists the number of citizens you can see at any time, of course, because it is always there in the bottom-right of your screen. This figure shows a wide disparity in pay, which means someone is getting paid a lot, or someone else very little. Check into such situations. You can probably raise the happiness of a whole building full of workers by increasing their pay.

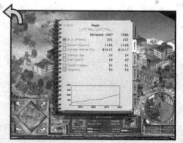

The People page of the almanac.

The people page also shows you the average worker pay, which isn't nearly as helpful as monitoring the relative pay for crucial jobs, as discussed earlier. It does show you the average age of your people, the quality of their food, and the average of their effects and happiness.

All right, let's click the Lists tab so we can find that income discrepancy mentioned earlier.

This is one of the most useful pages for monitoring your people. If you click on pay, you can see what all of your workers are being paid. Sometimes there are so many different pay rates that the pay page extends to two or more pages.

The lists page.

In this example, the engineers are being paid far in excess of what they would expect to have, and a quick check of the almanac shows that there were a number of farmers being paid less than what farmers elsewhere make. By clicking on an individual farmer from this screen, their job and house information appears.

Wow—those engineers are making $45 a month.

Whether or not you correct the income discrepancy depends upon how you desire to run your island. An unskilled worker has fewer options than an educated worker, who can simply leave the island. That is, unless you have an immigration office and set it to Nobody here gets out alive.

Two pages over, the farmers are only pulling down $9 dollars a month.

From the Lists page of the almanac, you can also monitor a number of important items—how many Tropicans belong to each faction. It is important to please the largest factions, is it not, el Presidente?

Many are content, some are happy, but four adults are displeased.

The Lists page also enables you to monitor the happiness of your people. By selecting the happiness attribute, you can see how many of your people are content, happy, or unhappy. The larger the number who are unhappy, the more trouble you may soon experience. It is usually wise to click on the individual unhappy people and see what it is they crave. Sometimes there is a little farm you neglected to give a raise; other times the person may be a rebel in waiting.

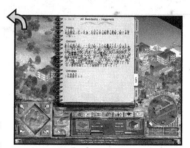

Diana Sadon's unhappiness may stem from her feelings about her job. Her unhappiness is so low that it barely registers.

The Age page is a vital one to monitor as well. From here, you can see whether or not college-educated workers are nearing retirement age. You can also see how many Tropicans will be joining the work force in the near future. Do they have a high school yet so that you can use them in industry? Young workers are more inclined to pursue education than older workers. If there are lots of children approaching working age, build a high school quickly to educate them.

If a particular individual is interesting or looks to be a potential problem, select them and they will appear in the circle window. You should see an open lock at the bottom of the circle window. Do you want to keep an eye on this one, el Presidente? Click the lock, and you can monitor them even after you exit the almanac.

Click the "lock" button if you want to keep watching the individual in question.

Other options on the Lists page enable you to look over the national origin, gender and the respect each person feels for you.

MONITORING THE INDIVIDUAL

Naturally, a ruler as astute as you knows other ways of keeping tabs on the people. Do you wish to look over the people at any building? Click on a building. You will see a row of people employed there, as well as how much money they make.

By clicking on an individual worker and then selecting the Job and House icon, you can see what their relative pay is (in comparison to workers with similar jobs outside Tropico). It's crucial that you keep an eye on this number for those with important jobs. If you want your people to be content, you should monitor relative pay for all jobs, but some important jobs are more important than others, yes?

You can see the income of your workers on this screen.

For example, early on you should take good care of your construction workers and dock workers to keep them happy, and therefore busier. Later on, when you get skilled workers, pay them well so that they stay at their current occupation.

Monitoring relative pay.

To see someone's skill level, select the individual and click the mortarboard. You can also take a look at the thoughts of your people by clicking on the Thoughts icon. Many of them are amusing—your little people, they are so simple.

Courtesy of the thought police, straight to you.

By clicking on the Happiness icon, you can see that Juan is feeling pretty good about his job, liberty, food, housing, and crime safety. Unfortunately, some of his other ratings are a little low, thus lowering his overall happiness. Tropico, love it or leave it Juan!

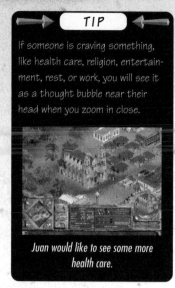

TIP

If someone is craving something, like health care, religion, entertainment, rest, or work, you will see it as a thought bubble near their head when you zoom in close.

Juan would like to see some more health care.

The Politics icon enables you to see what factions your people belong to, while the Family icon lets you know whether or not someone is married or has children.

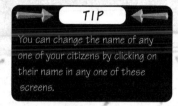

TIP

You can change the name of any one of your citizens by clicking on their name in any one of these screens.

The icon on the far-left is the Overview icon, which enables you to watch someone's overall feelings about their wants and needs, as well as their age. Watching age is very important for skilled workers, although this is naturally much easier to do with the almanac (you would need to click on many buildings to monitor them this way).

If your island doesn't have a college and all of your electric power plant workers are aging, you may be in a world of hurt. Yes, muchacho, if they leave the job, then you will have rolling blackouts until a replacement comes, and it will be many weeks before someone arrives by ship.

Pablo is nearing retirement age.

SALARIES

Let's say you've decided that your farmers are simply too unhappy with their lot. You're afraid rebellion may be in the air. First, select a farmer and check out her job quality rating to verify she's unhappy with her pay (oh—you wish to pay them that many peso? They will love you, el Presidente).

You may want to increase the salary only at an individual building (such as a crucial tobacco farm, or a farm that is experiencing difficulty attracting workers). If that's the case, simply click on the coin you wish to raise the wage to. If, however, you want to raise the wages at all your farms, press and hold the Shift key before clicking and the pay for every farm will increase.

If you want to give everyone in that same working class a raise (uneducated, high school, or college), then press and hold the Control key and click. It is like magic, your Excellency. Raising pay is one of the fastest ways to please your people.

Suppose that you need to fire someone. This can be a bad idea, el Presidente, as you do not need enemies, but sometimes this is necessary. Suppose that your new cigar plant has little tobacco with which to work, but is fully staffed. You are losing money! If you do not think tobacco supplies will increase soon, press Shift + Click to fire the worker. Upon doing so, click on the resulting empty space to block others from taking the vacated post.

A line of workers and their salary.

EMPTY SPACES

Certain buildings have more than empty spaces for their employees—they have empty spaces representing the number of people that can be served by each employee. Churches, clinics, pubs, and many other buildings cater to Tropicans, and if you don't have enough employees, a smaller number of people can use the service.

The number of people who can use the service is proportional to the number of employees working there. A church with a maximum number of priests (four) can handle 12 visitors. If you have half the number of employees, then you can only accomodate 6 visitors. It will do you no good at all to build a church if you have no one to staff it, and your health care will suffer if you have only one doctor in your clinic or hospital.

If there were another doctor in this clinic, four more people could be treated.

UNEDUCATED WORKERS

Tropico swarms with the uneducated, and many other uneducated people are eager to come to our island paradise. Any time you create a new building with jobs for the uneducated, the job will usually be filled quickly—as long as there is housing reasonably close and the pay is at least as good as other available jobs.

Following is a chart listing the types of jobs that can be held by uneducated workers.

UNEDUCATED

Job	Places Worked
Attendant	Beach site, Pool, Scenic outlook, Spa
Barmaid	Nightclub, Pub
Cook	Gourmet Restaurant, Restaurant
Dockworker	Dock
Farmer	Farm, Ranch
Fisherman	Fisherman's wharf
Laborer	Construction office

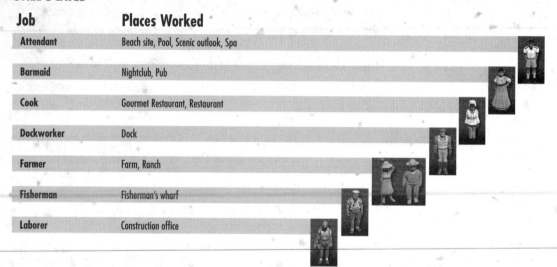

Job	Places Worked
Lumberjack	Logging camp
Maid	Bungalow, Cheap motel, Hotel, Luxury hotel
Miner	Mine
Showgirl	Cabaret
Teamster	Teamster's office

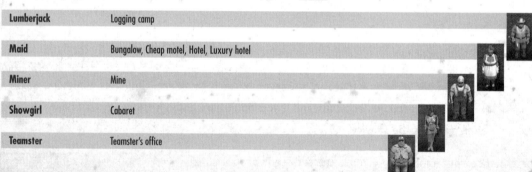

While any uneducated worker can fill these jobs, experience does count. Hold onto your experienced workers in key jobs, because they'll make your job simpler. You can do so by paying them well and generally making them content.

An experienced worker tries to stay in a job in which he or she is experienced, although this can be problematic. If for years you have multiple farms and only one construction office, and then you build several more construction offices, farmers are unlikely to accept the new jobs unless they pay twice as good as the farming job.

So what are the key positions? An el tigre such as yourself may find the showgirls very key indeed, but key positions really depend upon your goals. Generally speaking, any strategy requires building, so you should take good care of your laborers. You'll also need teamsters and dock workers to haul goods to the docks and onto freighters. If you have a great vein of gold, pay those miners well.

HIGH SCHOOL EDUCATED WORKERS

You don't start the game with many high school educated workers at all, save for those in a few key positions—your soldiers, for instance, and perhaps a bureaucrat if you started the game with the diplomat advantage.

The first two buildings you're likely to construct that require high school educated workers are the church, and the high school. Keep in mind that any building that requires someone with a high school education will likely stand empty. You just don't have anyone with the skills for the job, and skilled workers just don't drop into Tropico, not at the start of the game when your island has little to offer.

Click the mortarboard in the high school to hire more teachers. A ship icon appears—one's on the way!

To entice the high school educated workers to your tropical heaven, click on the blue mortarboard once the building that requires them is built. You'll pay a fee, but they'll arrive by ship. Avoid clicking the mortarboard when the building is first under way, or they may come and leave since there is nothing for them to do. You'll then end up paying another fee to lure another worker! Wait until just before the building is finished before clicking the mortarboard.

Of course, buildings that require high school educated workers usually must staff a number of them. If you want a full staff and you don't have a high school, you must continue to click on the blue mortarboard to get more from overseas and the prices climb quickly. Ay caramba!

Moreover, the cost of both types of foreign immigrants increases whenever you hire any foreign immigrant. So, if you hire 5 high school educated people early on, you've not only increased the cost of future high school immigrants, but also foreign immigrants with college degrees.

It's worth stating again that building a high school is a good thing. Build one early on, recruit some teachers, and then native Tropicans can fill the factory jobs, shop jobs, police posts, and so on.

HIGH SCHOOL EDUCATED

Job	Places Worked
Athlete	Sports complex
Bureaucrat	Immigration office, Diplomatic ministry
Factory Worker	Cannery, Cigar factory, Jewelry factory, Lumber mill, Rum distillery
Pit Boss	Casino
Policeman	Police office, Prison
Priest	Church
Shopkeeper	Market, Souvenir shop
Soldier	Palace, Guard post
Teacher	High school

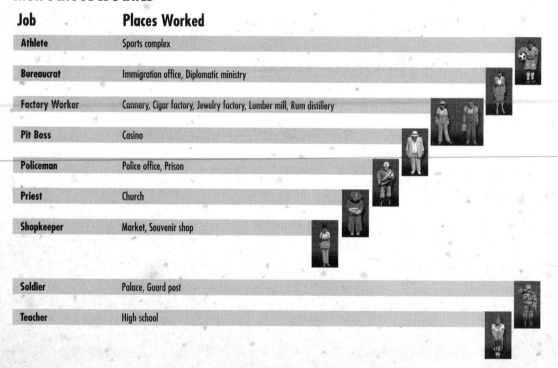

COLLEGE EDUCATED WORKERS

If high school educated workers are rare in Tropico, college educated workers are rarer still. At the start of the game, you're unlikely to have any people with a college education. If you do, they aren't working in jobs that require college degrees.

The first building you're likely to build that requires someone with a college education is a bank. Remember that you can use banks to give you a discount on building, as well as tucking money into your Swiss bank account. You're next most likely to require a doctor for you clinic, but probably won't have need for most of the other workers until your population climbs, you have a tourist paradise, or until its time for electricity.

Upon constructing a building that requires college educated workers, you can lure them from overseas by clicking the green mortarboard icon. You're then asked whether or not you want to pay the fee, or reminded gently that you don't have that amount left in your treasury.

Hiring a new banker requires $5,100 this time around.

Hiring college educated workers from overseas is more expensive than hiring high school educated workers, and the more you hire, the more expensive things get.

Take a look at the following chart. If you need half or more of these kinds of buildings, consider building a college so you can supply them with native Tropicans. Don't rush out and build a college too early in the game (well, you can't anyway—you must first build a high school). Wait until you are close to building your industries that will require the college educated, or already have some in place with some vacancies.

COLLEGE EDUCATED

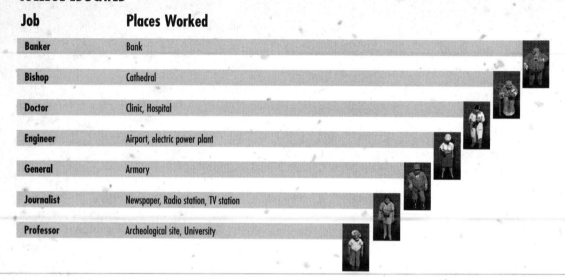

Job	Places Worked
Banker	Bank
Bishop	Cathedral
Doctor	Clinic, Hospital
Engineer	Airport, electric power plant
General	Armory
Journalist	Newspaper, Radio station, TV station
Professor	Archeological site, University

OTHER PEOPLE

El Presidente, as you wander our sunny tropical island you may encounter other people. You will find information about the tourists in a later chapter about tourism and industry.

You will also see students, mothers, children, retirees, the unemployed, and, unfortunately, rebels.

OTHERS

Job	Description
Student	Students attend schools so that they can learn more skills for the betterment of your pocketbook... eh, Tropico's economy.
Mothers	Some mothers are too busy with children and babies to do any work for Tropico. Mothers return to work when their youngest child is at least 8-years-old.
Children	Children play about the island until the age of thirteen, at which time you promptly put them to work.
Retirees	Retired Tropicans wander the island enjoying themselves.
Unemployed	If your economy booms you will not see many of the unemployed, your Excellency. They wander the island until a job is available.
Rebels	You will not be able to see the rebels unless they are near the city or attacking it! The rest of the time, the miserable cowards hide in the jungles.

Why do some people pursue an education while others prefer illiteracy? No one will pursue an education unless there are good paying jobs available that require an education. (The jobs must be gender-appropriate as well.) In addition, the resident must be of at least below average intelligence or better to attend high school and average intelligence for college. Lastly, the young and unskilled are more likely to attend school than older workers who have mastered a craft.

BUILDINGS & STRUCTURES

> "To sow schools is to reap men."
>
> —Castro

Tropico's previous rulers didn't have much use for buildings, and that is where you differ with them, el supremo! The strategy of a wise ruler such as yourself will largely depend upon what buildings you construct, and where and when you construct them.

Each building is listed in this chapter with its characteristics and costs, along with information on who can work there. In addition, it shows whether or not there are upgrades to improve the production quality or happiness of workers and many other factors.

After constructing a building, you can click on it at any time to see how much profit (or loss) it garners, along with other important statistics. For example, clicking on a church or cathedral enables you to see how many people have visited and what the quality of the service has been. Clicking on a high school or college enables you to see how many people have been educated there, and how efficient the institution is at its job.

The bishops in this cathedral obviously know their job. Their service quality is in the 90s.

Many buildings have crime, pollution, and beauty factors. If a beauty factor is in the negative, consider planting some inexpensive landscaping around the structure before the environmentalists come calling. This is important to consider if you want tourists to visit. Landscaping can also counteract unattractive buildings, although many buildings will require many pesos worth of landscaping before they are tolerable.

In general, proper layout of buildings is essential. While many buildings have detrimental effects on nearby buildings, keeping buildings close together reduces travel time and enables your people to be served by a smaller number of police stations, marketplaces, etc.

Less easy to fix is a building's pollution or crime score. Before you build industry, zoom out to watch which way the clouds blow, and then build your industries so that they don't blow pollution over the city. As far as crime, well, hire policemen and consider keeping nicer buildings far from ones that attract a criminal element. Basically, don't put your luxury hotel next to the tenements.

Every building has certain elements in common. Click on any building to see numbers representing wages paid out, the cost of maintenance, and the profit the building has generated. A school doesn't generate profit, but a factory does—if you're not paying out too much in wages or maintenance. Different kinds of buildings indicate other statistics. For example, a restaurant would show a quality of service rating. Naturally, the higher the number the better. Better quality buildings have higher ratings than cheaper buildings, and more experienced workers boost ratings as well.

You can raise or lower wages by clicking on the coins in the wage area. You can hire an educated worker from overseas by clicking on a mortarboard icon, if the building has one (blue requires a high school educated worker, green requires a college educated worker. Be warned, though, that hiring from overseas can be expensive). Buildings that service people (like schools and restaurants) show blank spots indicating how many people it can serve (unless there are people within the building currently being served). If these spots are crossed out with a large X, the crossed out spots can't be served until more staff is hired.

Most buildings have a selection near it that enables you to set other options for the building. For example, by clicking on the arrow in the sample screenshot above, you can set the school for general education, religious education, and parochial education. Other buildings have optional upgrades that you can select.

All buildings show a row of staffers currently working there, or a blank row indicating potential workers. You can fire a worker by selecting a worker and pressing the Shift key while clicking. You can keep empty positions empty by clicking on them, or open them back up by clicking on the next position to the right (or if only the final position is crossed out, by clicking it).

Reading the pollution or crime score is a bit different from the beauty score. Crime and pollution scores radiate. If the crime range indicates 10, then crime radiates in about 10 shack lengths in a circle around the building. A tenement with a crime range of 20 casts a long shadow, so any houses you build near them aren't likely to attract upscale residents.

You will also see a value listed as construction points. Each of your builders can work only so fast, depending upon their experience level. An inexperienced worker can only construct at a rate of 5 points per hammer stroke, while your most experienced workers can build at a rate of almost 23!

Of course, all this is offset by the distance from the work site to their home and office. Basically, commuting time cuts into their working time. And if you build on a grade, the land *must* be leveled. (Note that both inexperienced and experienced workers level ground at the same rate.)

INFRASTRUCTURE

Without your infrastructure, nothing on the island runs. You need a good infrastructure, el Presidente, although you need some things more than others. Banks, for instance, do more than just house money (they can funnel it!); use them for discounts on building expenses. Construction offices are a must-have, but airports aren't needed by just anyone.

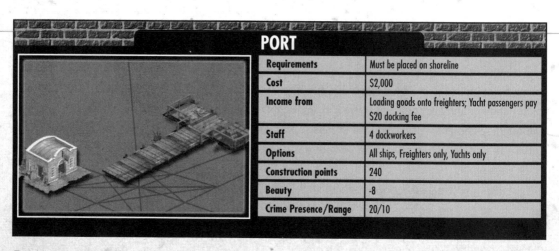

PORT

Requirements	Must be placed on shoreline
Cost	$2,000
Income from	Loading goods onto freighters; Yacht passengers pay $20 docking fee
Staff	4 dockworkers
Options	All ships, Freighters only, Yachts only
Construction points	240
Beauty	-8
Crime Presence/Range	20/10

Docks are ugly, crime-ridden areas throughout most of the world, even in sunny Tropico. If you decide to build a dock for yachts only, make sure you beautify the landscape and build it near a police station.

While having many docks may seem like a good thing—the more docks you have, the more goods that get shipped out—docks located next to each other rarely do much good.

If more than 30 units of trade goods are gathering dust on the dock, it may be time to build another one. However, you should consider putting it in another location, as near as possible to your industries. If it seems like your dock workers take a long time to move their goods, select them and see where they live. If they live far from the docks, build some housing for them that is closer to work.

AIRPORT

Cost	$16,000
Income From	$100 for coach tickets, $200 for first-class tickets
Staff	2 engineers (college educated)
Upgrades	*Enhanced terminal:* $6,000 (2 planes can use the airport at once) *Control tower:* $8,000 + 10 Mw electricity (larger planes, with up to 2/3 more passengers, can land at the airport)
Options	Coach service, first-class service
Construction Points	1000
Beauty	-8

You probably don't need to consider an airport unless your tourism industry is thriving and you have a lot of money. Take a close look at the construction points required to build an airport. It will take your workers a long time to complete the job, especially if your workers must travel far to the job site. Build a construction office and cheap housing by the airport to increase efficiency.

TEAMSTER'S OFFICE

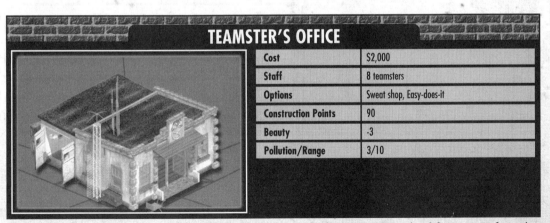

Cost	$2,000
Staff	8 teamsters
Options	Sweat shop, Easy-does-it
Construction Points	90
Beauty	-3
Pollution/Range	3/10

Most games start with a teamster's office already in place. A teamster can haul five units of goods at a time, compared to a regular worker who can haul two. This relieves the farmers and other workers from having to haul so that they can tend to their own goods.

If you notice someone other than a teamster pushing a wheelbarrow around, hire some more teamsters or build another teamster's office.

CONSTRUCTION OFFICE

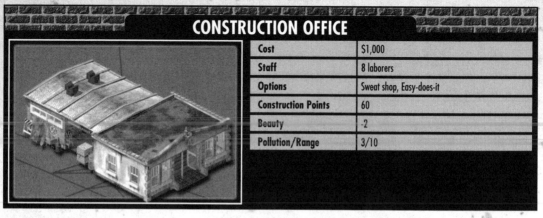

Cost	$1,000
Staff	8 laborers
Options	Sweat shop, Easy-does-it
Construction Points	60
Beauty	-2
Pollution/Range	3/10

It may be a little ugly, but you can spruce up the outside with a little landscaping. Construction offices are some of the most useful buildings in the game. Without construction offices, nothing else gets built. Plan on building an extra one soon after you start the game, and build more as your city grows so that buildings can rise more quickly.

If you have a new crop of buildings you plan to construct, build a new construction site beside them first so that your builders won't have as far to walk.

ELECTRIC POWER PLANT

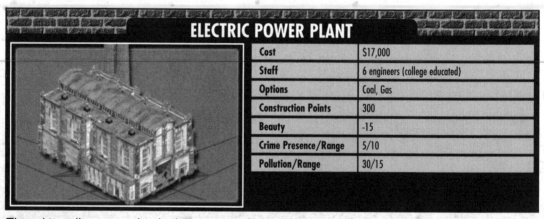

Cost	$17,000
Staff	6 engineers (college educated)
Options	Coal, Gas
Construction Points	300
Beauty	-15
Crime Presence/Range	5/10
Pollution/Range	30/15

These big polluters may be the keys to your future. Without them, you just can't build some of the nicest (and priciest) structures and without those structures, your reign will likely end sooner than it might have.

Monitor the age and happiness levels of your engineers, as well as the power output. If you're running close to maximum usage and a worker retires or quits, you're in for rolling blackouts until a new worker is imported (muy expensivo) or joins (you do have a college, right?). Try to always have more power than you need to help buffer this situation. If blackouts cause power loss to the hospital or luxury hotel, then some of your ratings will drop and take a while to recoup.

Also, keep a close eye on your power grid, which you can do by clicking on your power plant. Everything in green is within your power grid. If you need to add buildings with electricity outside the grid and you have enough power, build a sub station.

TIP

Gas doubles maintenance cost, but lowers pollution by 50%.

ELECTRIC SUBSTATION

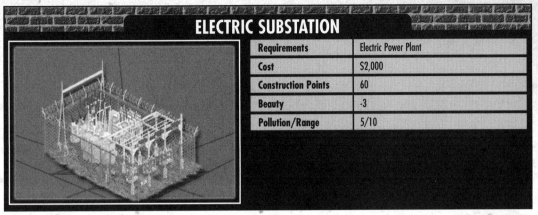

Requirements	Electric Power Plant
Cost	$2,000
Construction Points	60
Beauty	-3
Pollution/Range	5/10

These structures aren't mini-power stations—they merely extend your power grid. (See the electric power plant entry for more information.) Place it just inside the outer edge of your current power grid to extend it further.

BANK

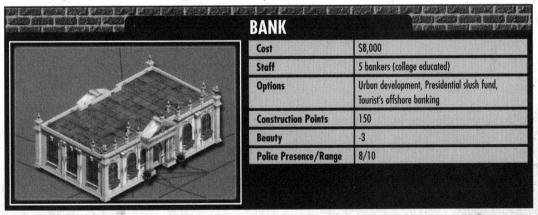

Cost	$8,000
Staff	5 bankers (college educated)
Options	Urban development, Presidential slush fund, Tourist's offshore banking
Construction Points	150
Beauty	-3
Police Presence/Range	8/10

If you want to make money, or want to make your people happy by building them lots of things, build a bank early on. By setting a bank for the urban development option, you receive a discount on buildings that you buy. The effect is cumulative: the more banks you have, the greater the effect, although you won't get more than a 40% discount, so plan on four or five eventually, not 10, because the effect levels off.

If you want to build your Swiss bank account, don't forget the presidential slush fund, which helps money flow into el Presidente's coffers. Also, when the wealthy tourists arrive in droves (don't bother doing this with the cheap tourists!), make sure you set up some banks with tourist's offshore banking to bring more money to Tropico.

HOUSING

Housing is one of the major concerns of your people, and it's a small wonder. When the game starts, everyone is living in squalid shacks comprised of whatever jetsam they could gather together. You should get them out of shacks as soon as possible, even if you're not worried about their well being. Keeping your citizens in shacks is just asking for a revolution. Besides, you can charge them rent in anything else.

The homes are graded by quality, in the following order. Naturally, everyone would love to live in a luxury home, but those require a higher rent payment, not to mention electricity. Electricity! What will they think of next?

- Shack
- Bunkhouse
- Tenement
- Country House
- Apartment Complex
- House
- Luxury House

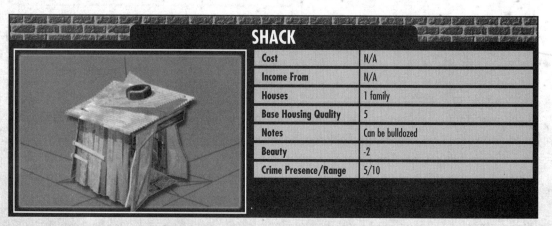

SHACK

Cost	N/A
Income From	N/A
Houses	1 family
Base Housing Quality	5
Notes	Can be bulldozed
Beauty	-2
Crime Presence/Range	5/10

When the game starts, your people have only these eyesores to live in and they're not happy about it. Any time you run low on housing, shacks start appearing all over the place, sometimes in inconvenient places (for example, next to your luxury hotels).

You can bulldoze shacks, but remember that it takes time for your construction crew to build (or destroy) anything, especially if they're busy erecting el Presidente's new nightclub. Once abandoned, shacks will deteriorate into rubble in a year. Build new housing, wait for the abandoned shacks to collapse, save your bulldozing money, and simply clean up the rubble.

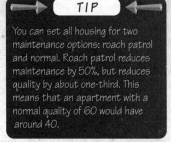

TIP

You can set all housing for two maintenance options: roach patrol and normal. Roach patrol reduces maintenance by 50%, but reduces quality by about one-third. This means that an apartment with a normal quality of 60 would have around 40.

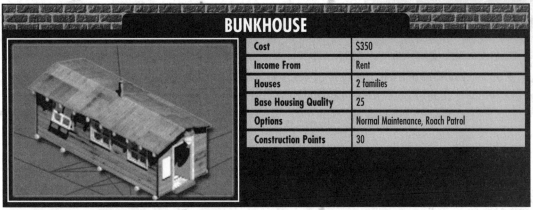

BUNKHOUSE

Cost	$350
Income From	Rent
Houses	2 families
Base Housing Quality	25
Options	Normal Maintenance, Roach Patrol
Construction Points	30

Bunkhouses have a number of things going for them: They're cheap, you can put them up quick, and they are far better than shacks. If your citizens are angry about living in shacks, just construct a bunch of bunkhouses. They won't be delighted, but they'll be further from revolt.

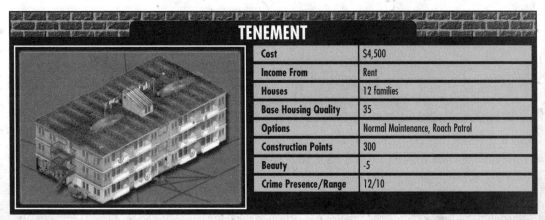

TENEMENT

Cost	$4,500
Income From	Rent
Houses	12 families
Base Housing Quality	35
Options	Normal Maintenance, Roach Patrol
Construction Points	300
Beauty	-5
Crime Presence/Range	12/10

Tenement apartments are cheap and house many families, but they are also ugly and attract crime. Plus, they don't really make the people living in them all that happy, if that's something that concerns you.

Remember that if you start as a diplomat, you get a foreign ministry at the beginning of the game. With that in place, you can select the foreign policy edict Russian Developmental Aid and build tenements and apartment complexes at half cost! Of course, you need to have good relations with the Russians. For more information, see the Edicts chapter.

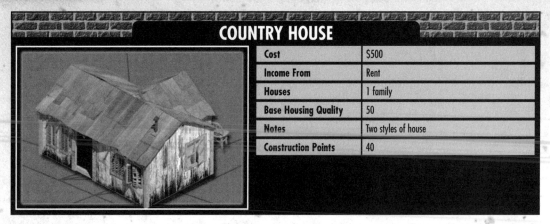

COUNTRY HOUSE

Cost	$500
Income From	Rent
Houses	1 family
Base Housing Quality	50
Notes	Two styles of house
Construction Points	40

The country houses are half the cost of a regular house, but seem to produce a little less happiness amongst your people than building regular houses and even apartments.

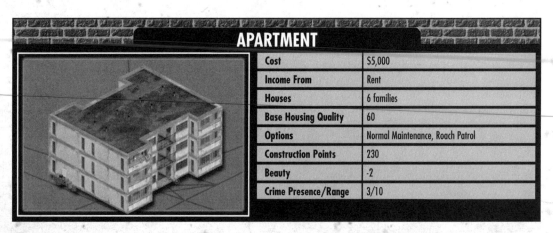

APARTMENT

Cost	$5,000
Income From	Rent
Houses	6 families
Base Housing Quality	60
Options	Normal Maintenance, Roach Patrol
Construction Points	230
Beauty	-2
Crime Presence/Range	3/10

This is it—they may be a little ugly and a little crime prone, but they're the best thing most Tropicans can hope to live in. If you want your people happy with housing, most will be delighted when you erect apartments for them.

HOUSE

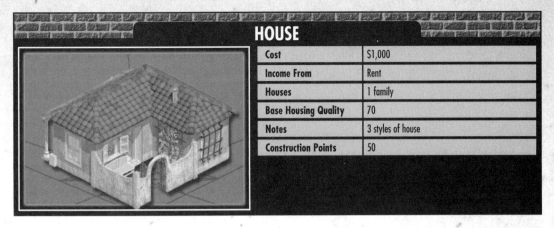

Cost	$1,000
Income From	Rent
Houses	1 family
Base Housing Quality	70
Notes	3 styles of house
Construction Points	50

Tropicans love having homes of their own and will flock to them as soon as you construct them. Until you have electricity, these are the best accommodations anyone can have—except for your glorious self, el Presidente!

LUXURY HOUSE

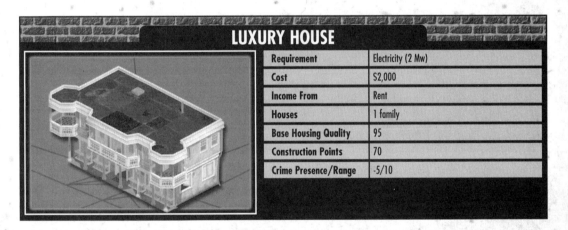

Requirement	Electricity (2 Mw)
Cost	$2,000
Income From	Rent
Houses	1 family
Base Housing Quality	95
Construction Points	70
Crime Presence/Range	-5/10

Naturally, anyone who cannot live in your splendid palace would love a fine, luxury home of their own, but they require electricity and come with a hefty price tag. As you can see, they are so imposing and splendid that they actually discourage criminals from coming near.

However, this should not be taken as an invitation to build your luxury homes near the slums! Erect them near the workplaces of your college educated workers, and raise the rent—they can afford it! Luxury houses are especially useful for keeeping generals happy.

SIMPLE INDUSTRY

Farming, ranching, fishing, logging, and mining are the simpler industries you need to get your island running. Regardless of whether you want your island to be an environmental paradise or an economic powerhouse, you need food for your people and you need money for your workers.

Heavy industry depends upon the raw materials produced by simple industry and cannot exist without it. Don't be fooled by the term simple, though, because many of these products are very lucrative. In deference to the capitalist dogs, these industries are listed by cost, cheapest first.

RANCH

Cost	$750
Income From	Raising livestock
Staff	2 farmers
Upgrades	*Smokehouse:* $2,000 (+20% profit for smoked beef, but not smoked goat)
Options	Cattle, goats
Notes	Build ranch on grazing land
Construction Points	80
Beauty	-3
Pollution/Range	5/10

As you might expect, goats can find nourishment on about any terrain. Finding a good site for cattle, though, can be tricky on an island with high elevation.

Make sure you check the terrain before building your ranch, and avoid building near the tourists. They probably won't want to watch the goats and cattle from their gourmet restaurant.

It takes a while for a ranch to turn a profit (the herd must multiply). But after 5 or 10 years, ranches can be quite profitable. Plus, they require only two workers.

FARM

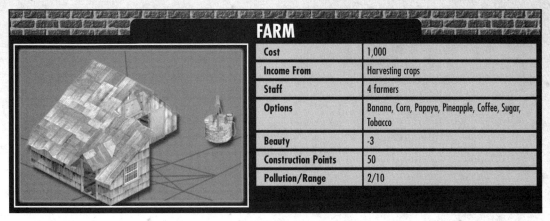

Cost	1,000
Income From	Harvesting crops
Staff	4 farmers
Options	Banana, Corn, Papaya, Pineapple, Coffee, Sugar, Tobacco
Beauty	-3
Construction Points	50
Pollution/Range	2/10

Before choosing your crop, make sure you know where to grow it. Cycle through the farms to see where the best sites for each type are located. Remember that coffee, sugar, and tobacco are cash crops and won't feed your people! On the other hand, corn and papaya are best used for food. You can use pineapples and bananas a food source *and* a cash crop—they're good for both.

It takes about three years to grow cash crops. Food crops typically produce food in about two years (five years for the tree crops of bananas and papayas).

LOGGING CAMP

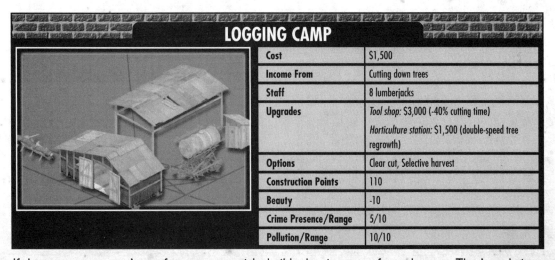

Cost	$1,500
Income From	Cutting down trees
Staff	8 lumberjacks
Upgrades	*Tool shop:* $3,000 (-40% cutting time)
	Horticulture station: $1,500 (double-speed tree regrowth)
Options	Clear cut, Selective harvest
Construction Points	110
Beauty	-10
Crime Presence/Range	5/10
Pollution/Range	10/10

If the tree groves aren't too far away, you might build a logging camp from the start. They're relatively cheap and they earn money. Remember, though, that too much logging can anger the environmental faction and cause problems with the tourist trade because of the pollution and loss of beauty.

FISHERMAN'S WHARF

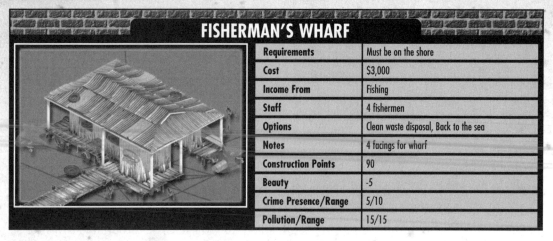

Requirements	Must be on the shore
Cost	$3,000
Income From	Fishing
Staff	4 fishermen
Options	Clean waste disposal, Back to the sea
Notes	4 facings for wharf
Construction Points	90
Beauty	-5
Crime Presence/Range	5/10
Pollution/Range	15/15

Fisherman's wharves are a good food source, but are a big polluter and fish aren't worth many yanqui dollars unless canned. Avoid building anywhere near a potential tourist attraction. These can be useful if land is scarce and you have a large population to feed.

MINE

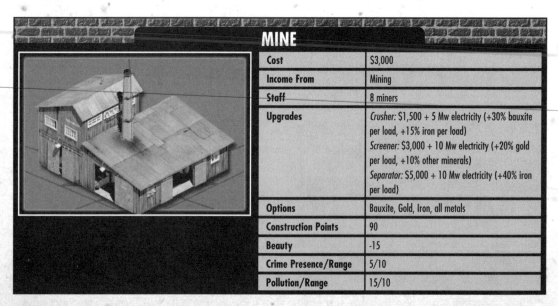

Cost	$3,000
Income From	Mining
Staff	8 miners
Upgrades	*Crusher:* $1,500 + 5 Mw electricity (+30% bauxite per load, +15% iron per load) *Screener:* $3,000 + 10 Mw electricity (+20% gold per load, +10% other minerals) *Separator:* $5,000 + 10 Mw electricity (+40% iron per load)
Options	Bauxite, Gold, Iron, all metals
Construction Points	90
Beauty	-15
Crime Presence/Range	5/10
Pollution/Range	15/10

Before you build mines, check the terrain for minerals and ensure you build the right kind of mine at the right location. A bauxite mine is no good on top of an iron deposit.

Avoid building a bauxite mine close to city center or iron, for that matter, unless you have few other options. However, you should mine gold wherever you can find it.

INDUSTRIAL STRUCTURES

It is your destiny to guide your island into a glorious future and to make many pesos. That's why you need industry. It's big, it's ugly, and it's not cheap, but if you build the right things in the right places, you will soon be lighting your cigars with 50-dollar yanqui notes.

All industry causes pollution, and all these buildings are eyesores. Crime rates tend to increase near industrial buildings as well, so don't plan a nice batch of luxury homes or tourist attractions anywhere near these areas.

Industry requires workers with a high school education. Even if your people's welfare isn't an immediate concern, you should invest in a local high school early on. It gets to be quite expensive hiring off-island labor.

For the benefit of the capitalists, the industries are ranked by price of construction. Generally, the more expensive an industry is to build, the more lucrative it is in the long run. Note that you can make the jewelry factory substantially more lucrative with the addition of the very expensive finishing shop, which requires electricity.

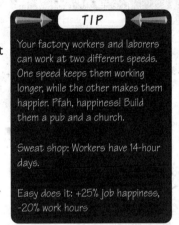

TIP

Your factory workers and laborers can work at two different speeds. One speed keeps them working longer, while the other makes them happier. Pfah, happiness! Build them a pub and a church.

Sweat shop: Workers have 14-hour days.

Easy does it: +25% job happiness, -20% work hours

LUMBER MILL

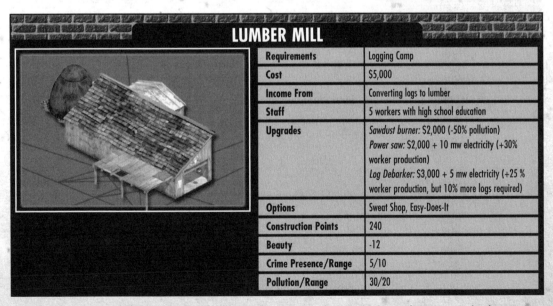

Requirements	Logging Camp
Cost	$5,000
Income From	Converting logs to lumber
Staff	5 workers with high school education
Upgrades	Sawdust burner: $2,000 (-50% pollution) Power saw: $2,000 + 10 mw electricity (+30% worker production) Log Debarker: $3,000 + 5 mw electricity (+25 % worker production, but 10% more logs required)
Options	Sweat Shop, Easy-Does-It
Construction Points	240
Beauty	-12
Crime Presence/Range	5/10
Pollution/Range	30/20

Naturally, you need logs before you can start processing them, which is why you need a logging camp before you build your lumber mill.

CIGAR FACTORY

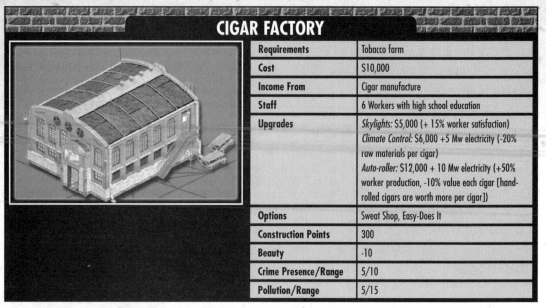

Requirements	Tobacco farm
Cost	$10,000
Income From	Cigar manufacture
Staff	6 Workers with high school education
Upgrades	*Skylights:* $5,000 (+ 15% worker satisfaction) *Climate Control:* $6,000 +5 Mw electricity (-20% raw materials per cigar) *Auto-roller:* $12,000 + 10 Mw electricity (+50% worker production, -10% value each cigar [hand-rolled cigars are worth more per cigar])
Options	Sweat Shop, Easy-Does It
Construction Points	300
Beauty	-10
Crime Presence/Range	5/10
Pollution/Range	5/15

Note that cigar factories pollute far less than any other industry, a mere 5, which is nothing compared to most of the other industries. Keep that bit of information in mind if you want an industry to build up your cash so that you can turn your island into a tourist's paradise. Also, remember that tobacco seems more inclined to flourish on Tropico than any other cash crop.

JEWELRY FACTORY

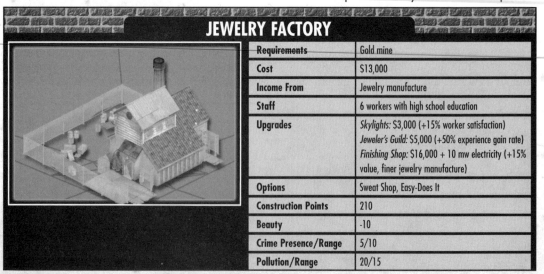

Requirements	Gold mine
Cost	$13,000
Income From	Jewelry manufacture
Staff	6 workers with high school education
Upgrades	*Skylights:* $3,000 (+15% worker satisfaction) *Jeweler's Guild:* $5,000 (+50% experience gain rate) *Finishing Shop:* $16,000 + 10 mw electricity (+15% value, finer jewelry manufacture)
Options	Sweat Shop, Easy-Does It
Construction Points	210
Beauty	-10
Crime Presence/Range	5/10
Pollution/Range	20/15

If you want to turn an even better profit with your gold mines—assuming you HAVE a gold mine—build a jewelry factory. Only buy the jeweler's guild early on; later in the game, the experience bonus won't have enough time to have an impact.

If you can spring for the finishing shop, do so. However, if you can't do that until later in the game (because of the electricity requirement), make sure your mine is still producing gold before you pay for it.

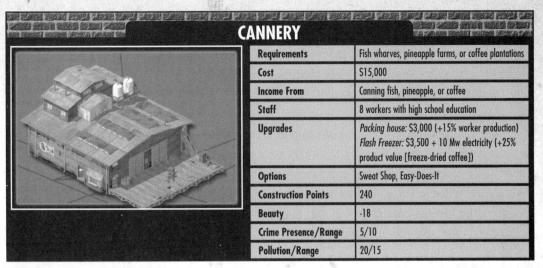

CANNERY

Requirements	Fish wharves, pineapple farms, or coffee plantations
Cost	$15,000
Income From	Canning fish, pineapple, or coffee
Staff	8 workers with high school education
Upgrades	*Packing house:* $3,000 (+15% worker production) *Flash Freezer:* $3,500 + 10 Mw electricity (+25% product value [freeze-dried coffee])
Options	Sweat Shop, Easy-Does-It
Construction Points	240
Beauty	-18
Crime Presence/Range	5/10
Pollution/Range	20/15

Canneries are especially ugly. It's important to note that a cannery doesn't do any good if you don't have pineapple farms, coffee farms, or fish wharves. If you have none of these, then you have nothing to can. Although canning fish does produce money, coffee and pineapple are more lucrative.

RUM DISTILLERY

Requirement	Sugarcane farms
Cost	$22,000
Income From	Refinement of sugar into rum
Staff	12 workers with high school education
Upgrades	*Flavoring facility:* $15,000 (+15% per barrel [spiced rum]) *Mulching Machinery:* $10,000 + 15 Mw electricity (+20% worker production)
Options	Sweat Shop, Easy-Does It
Construction Points	390
Beauty	-15
Crime Presence/Range	10/10
Pollution/Range	40/20

Want to make more profit from your sugar cane farms? Consider a rum distillery. They're big polluters, but rum brings in an especially nice profit, especially if you take the booze baron advantage at game startup.

Distilleries are best if there is a lot of available land for sugar. If it starts going well, especially with the booze baron, you can make lots of money.

ENTERTAINMENT

Your people, they work very hard, el Presidente. They need some places to go to relax, unwind, and keep them busy when they aren't working.

If you want content workers, you must construct entertainment at the beginning of the game. If your people are in the red about entertainment, constructing a pub and a restaurant doesn't fix the problem immediately. The unhappiness won't decrease until many islanders have had the opportunity to visit the entertainment options you offer, sometimes multiple times.

Entertainment is also a draw for tourists, who need some place to go besides beaches and scenic views when they visit exotic Tropico.

There is seldom a need to build duplicate structures. You are unlikely to need two pubs or restaurants. The locals and the tourists prefer a variety of options; build one of everything before doubling up.

Make sure you note that most of these structures increase the likelihood of crimes in nearby areas, so be careful where you place them.

TIP

There are certain options you will find in the buildings dedicated to entertainment. Here's what they do:

Paper placemats: Maintenance costs -30, quality -10

Cloth napkins: Normal maintenance and quality

Linen tablecloths: +50% maintenance costs, +10 % quality

No dress code: Anyone can enter, wearing just about anything. While this may please the locals, it won't attract wealthy tourists.

Upscale dress code: Keeps the riffraff out, limits clientele, but raises quality

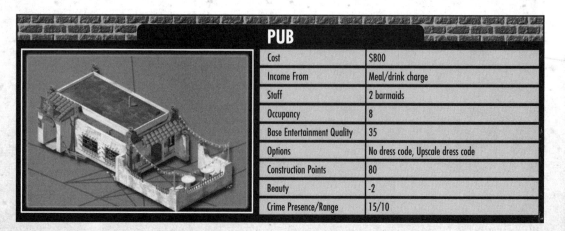

PUB

Cost	$800
Income From	Meal/drink charge
Staff	2 barmaids
Occupancy	8
Base Entertainment Quality	35
Options	No dress code, Upscale dress code
Construction Points	80
Beauty	-2
Crime Presence/Range	15/10

If you want your people happy, or merely content enough that they don't rebel, you should build a pub during your first few years in office.

RESTAURANT

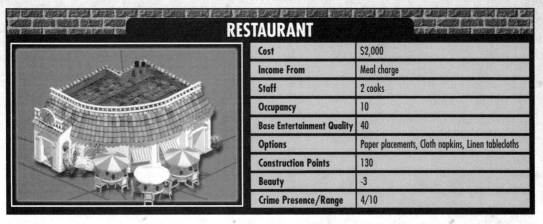

Cost	$2,000
Income From	Meal charge
Staff	2 cooks
Occupancy	10
Base Entertainment Quality	40
Options	Paper placements, Cloth napkins, Linen tablecloths
Construction Points	130
Beauty	-3
Crime Presence/Range	4/10

Since you feed your people so well, they have little need for restaurant food, but they do enjoy the entertainment offered at restaurants. Consider adding a restaurant to Tropico when your population nears 100, or even before.

NIGHTCLUB

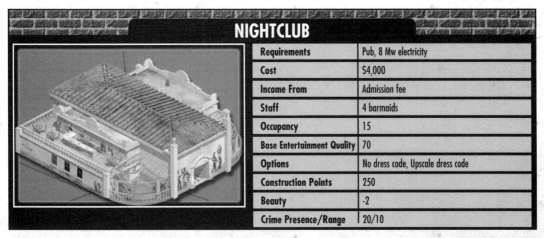

Requirements	Pub, 8 Mw electricity
Cost	$4,000
Income From	Admission fee
Staff	4 barmaids
Occupancy	15
Base Entertainment Quality	70
Options	No dress code, Upscale dress code
Construction Points	250
Beauty	-2
Crime Presence/Range	20/10

If you want Tropico to really swing, consider building a nightclub. It adds a new form of entertainment for Tropicans, and will be a draw for the tourists.

A nightclub serves as an improved pub, appealing to the same crowd who like to drink and have a good time.

Just make sure you look at the negative impact nightclubs have on crime and plan accordingly. Consider putting one near a police station or military outpost, or even a church.

GOURMET RESTAURANT

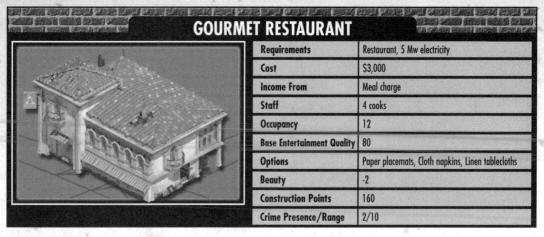

Requirements	Restaurant, 5 Mw electricity
Cost	$3,000
Income From	Meal charge
Staff	4 cooks
Occupancy	12
Base Entertainment Quality	80
Options	Paper placemats, Cloth napkins, Linen tablecloths
Beauty	-2
Construction Points	160
Crime Presence/Range	2/10

Until college-educated workers and tourists reach your island, a gourmet restaurant is an expensive luxury.

SPORTS COMPLEX

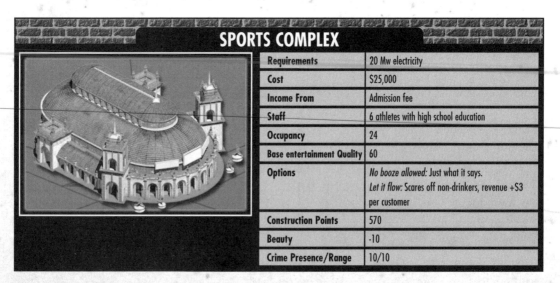

Requirements	20 Mw electricity
Cost	$25,000
Income From	Admission fee
Staff	6 athletes with high school education
Occupancy	24
Base entertainment Quality	60
Options	No booze allowed: Just what it says. Let it flow: Scares off non-drinkers, revenue +$3 per customer
Construction Points	570
Beauty	-10
Crime Presence/Range	10/10

When the island's population climbs and your tourist industry is good, an arena is a good entertainment draw and a good way to employ high school educated workers.

After building the sports complex, you can even host the Pan-Caribbean games and draw even more tourists to your isle.

CASINO

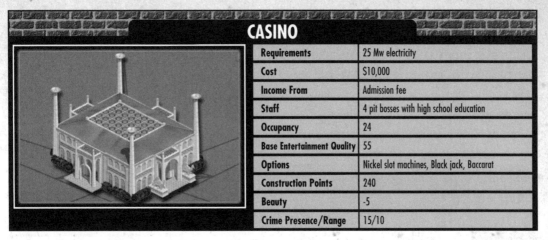

Requirements	25 Mw electricity
Cost	$10,000
Income From	Admission fee
Staff	4 pit bosses with high school education
Occupancy	24
Base Entertainment Quality	55
Options	Nickel slot machines, Black jack, Baccarat
Construction Points	240
Beauty	-5
Crime Presence/Range	15/10

You are not the only one who loves a good game of chance, el Presidente. Once you have electricity, build a casino. Your people and the tourists will come to spend their money, and there is always room for you at the table!

CABARET

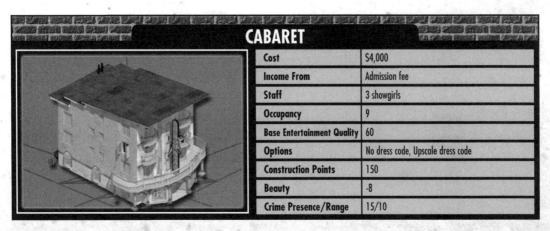

Cost	$4,000
Income From	Admission fee
Staff	3 showgirls
Occupancy	9
Base Entertainment Quality	60
Options	No dress code, Upscale dress code
Construction Points	150
Beauty	-8
Crime Presence/Range	15/10

It is strange, your excellency, but your people do not seem to appreciate the cabaret dancers as much as you do!

The cabaret rarely turns much profit, but it does keep the soldiers very happy, as well as other male workers. Priests frequent the cabaret as well, undoubtedly to hand out pamphlets.

TOURISM

Unless you want to only become an industrial powerhouse, you are likely to find some use for tourism. You can build a variety of tourist attractions to lure foreign money to your shores. All tourist structures attract criminals looking for easy money, so build a police station near your tourist attractions to counteract the slightly increased crime rate. Tourists can visit tourist attractions and regular entertainment; locals won't visit tourist sites.

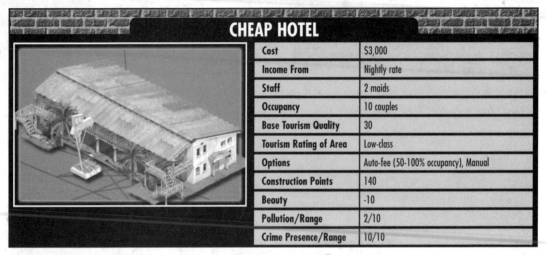

CHEAP HOTEL

Cost	$3,000
Income From	Nightly rate
Staff	2 maids
Occupancy	10 couples
Base Tourism Quality	30
Tourism Rating of Area	Low-class
Options	Auto-fee (50-100% occupancy), Manual
Construction Points	140
Beauty	-10
Pollution/Range	2/10
Crime Presence/Range	10/10

El Presidente, some tourists wish to stretch their money as far as it will go, and so they come to humble Tropico and stay in cheap hotels. Because these hotels produce some pollution and are an ugly sight, put some landscaping around them and don't build hotels or luxury hotels nearby.

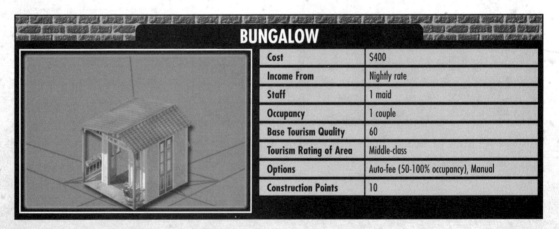

BUNGALOW

Cost	$400
Income From	Nightly rate
Staff	1 maid
Occupancy	1 couple
Base Tourism Quality	60
Tourism Rating of Area	Middle-class
Options	Auto-fee (50-100% occupancy), Manual
Construction Points	10

A simple bungalow, cheap to build and attractive to middle-class tourists. Don't build just one—construct multiple ones together and build a beach site nearby.

HOTEL

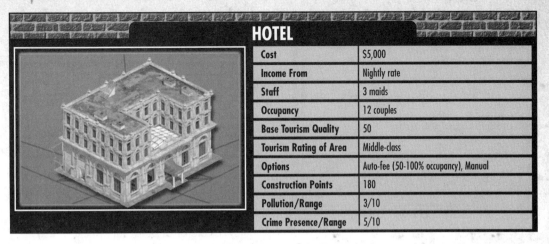

Cost	$5,000
Income From	Nightly rate
Staff	3 maids
Occupancy	12 couples
Base Tourism Quality	50
Tourism Rating of Area	Middle-class
Options	Auto-fee (50-100% occupancy), Manual
Construction Points	180
Pollution/Range	3/10
Crime Presence/Range	5/10

To get middle-class tourists, you must build better hotels. Beautify them with some landscaping, and make sure you build some attractions before you build the hotel or few will come.

LUXURY HOTEL

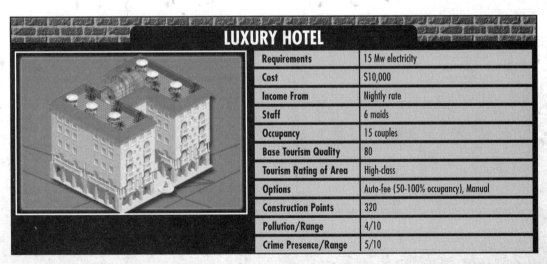

Requirements	15 Mw electricity
Cost	$10,000
Income From	Nightly rate
Staff	6 maids
Occupancy	15 couples
Base Tourism Quality	80
Tourism Rating of Area	High-class
Options	Auto-fee (50-100% occupancy), Manual
Construction Points	320
Pollution/Range	4/10
Crime Presence/Range	5/10

The foreign elite wants elegant accommodations. Don't just build this jewel, though—make sure you have other tourist attractions for them to visit first. Build a nearby dock solely for yachts, put in some landscaping, construct a police station, and so on.

BEACH SITE

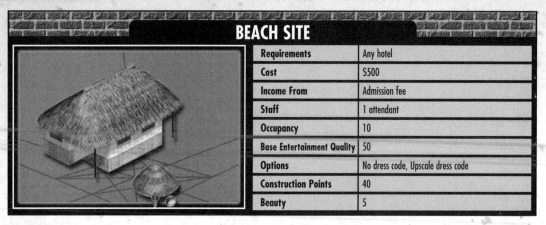

Requirements	Any hotel
Cost	$500
Income From	Admission fee
Staff	1 attendant
Occupancy	10
Base Entertainment Quality	50
Options	No dress code, Upscale dress code
Construction Points	40
Beauty	5

All tourists love beach sites, so build plenty of them. They're one of the best lures near cheap hotels.

SCENIC OUTLOOK

Requirements	Any hotel
Cost	$1,000
Income From	Admission fee
Staff	1 attendant
Occupancy	6
Base Entertainment Quality	50
Options	Mimeographed handout, 4-color brochure
Notes	Environmental quality very strong
Construction Points	40

If you build scenic outlooks, construct the outlook near something scenic! Put them near something beautiful, like an archeological site, a cathedral, the ocean, and put landscaping nearby.

SOUVENIR SHOP

Requirements	Any hotel
Cost	$1,250
Income From	Tourist purchases
Staff	2 shopkeepers with high school education
Occupancy	10
Base Entertainment Quality	35
Options	T-shirts, arts and crafts
Construction Points	80
Beauty	-2
Crime Presence/Range	2/10

If you have tourists, you need these. Where else can they buy their official Viva El Presidente T-shirts, Tropico flags, and painted clam shells?

ARCHEOLOGICAL SITE

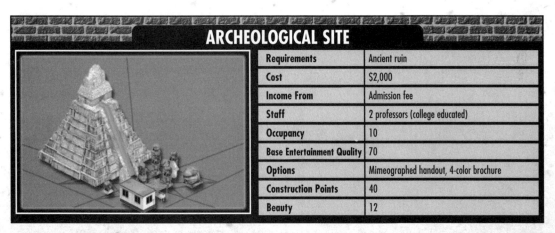

Requirements	Ancient ruin
Cost	$2,000
Income From	Admission fee
Staff	2 professors (college educated)
Occupancy	10
Base Entertainment Quality	70
Options	Mimeographed handout, 4-color brochure
Construction Points	40
Beauty	12

While you and I know that the ruins are merely a fine source of pre-cut stone, many abroad pay much money to view these old things. Who knows why? If they are so wonderful, why did the ancients move out?

POOL

Requirements	Any hotel
Cost	$4,000
Income From	Admission fee
Staff	2 attendants
Occupancy	16
Base Entertainment Quality	60
Options	No dress code, Upscale dress code
Construction Points	50
Crime Presence/Range	2/10

It seems strange, but the foreigners will pay much money to swim in a pool when there is a perfectly fine sea within a hundred feet. Note the dress code options, and plan on having an upscale dress code if you have hotels and luxury hotels.

SPA

Requirements	Any hotel
Cost	$5,000
Income From	Admission fee
Staff	3 attendants
Occupancy	9
Base Entertainment Quality	90
Options	No dress code, Upscale dress code
Construction Points	80
Crime Presence/Range	2/10

As you might guess (how clever you are, el Presidente!), spas cater to wealthier tourists and come with a stiff admission fee. The upscale dress code is highly suggested.

GOVERNMENT

You are the government, of course. These buildings merely enable you to better maintain your enlightened grip on the masses. Tropicans are proud of your splendid palace, so why not build them some jails and guard posts and spruce them up with some landscaping? They will surely be proud of them as well.

Diplomatic ministry's can be a boon to your realm early on, but you can postpone many of the other government structures for later in the game.

The effect of the media depends in no small part upon the experience of your journalists.

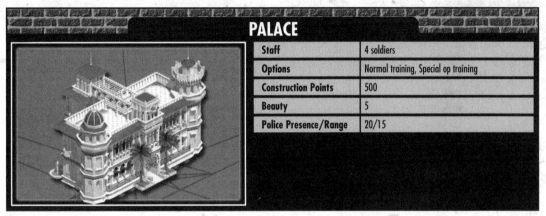

PALACE

Staff	4 soldiers
Options	Normal training, Special op training
Construction Points	500
Beauty	5
Police Presence/Range	20/15

Ah, home sweet home, and the loveliest residence on the island. Why not make it even more beautiful with some landscaping? Plant some trees and shrubs around your residence. Oh, and don't forget to pay your guards well, el Presidente.

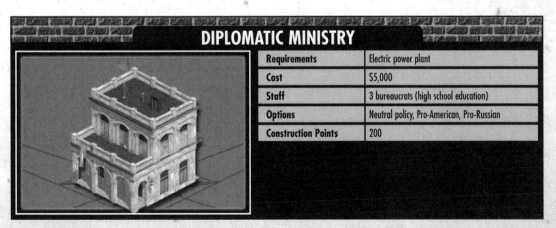

DIPLOMATIC MINISTRY

Requirements	Electric power plant
Cost	$5,000
Staff	3 bureaucrats (high school education)
Options	Neutral policy, Pro-American, Pro-Russian
Construction Points	200

A diplomatic ministry enables you to use the USA or the Russians as financial sources. Without a ministry, you can't enact any foreign policy edicts!

POLICE STATION

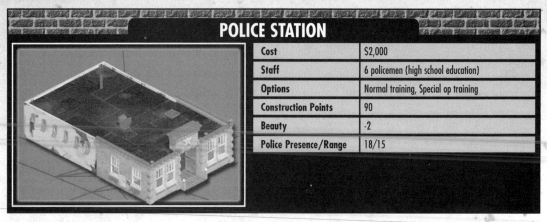

Cost	$2,000
Staff	6 policemen (high school education)
Options	Normal training, Special op training
Construction Points	90
Beauty	-2
Police Presence/Range	18/15

If you plan to develop a tourist's paradise, your tourists need to feel safe, so plan on a few of these once things really boom. On the other hand, you probably won't need a police station until 20 years or so into the game. Someone needs to keep down the crime near tenement buildings and factories.

PRISON

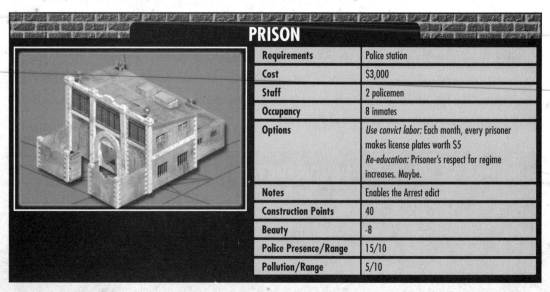

Requirements	Police station
Cost	$3,000
Staff	2 policemen
Occupancy	8 inmates
Options	*Use convict labor:* Each month, every prisoner makes license plates worth $5 *Re-education:* Prisoner's respect for regime increases. Maybe.
Notes	Enables the Arrest edict
Construction Points	40
Beauty	-8
Police Presence/Range	15/10
Pollution/Range	5/10

You may not need prisons unless your population is booming and tends to be unhappy. Truly, el Presidente, if Tropico is a paradise, who needs prisons? On the other hand, if your people do not understand your vision, prisons may be needed for their own good.

GUARD STATION

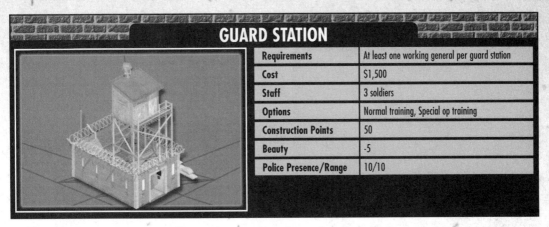

Requirements	At least one working general per guard station
Cost	$1,500
Staff	3 soldiers
Options	Normal training, Special op training
Construction Points	50
Beauty	-5
Police Presence/Range	10/10

If the rebels are giving you problems, then you need guard stations. Before you build any guard stations, though, you need generals so you must build armories first and hire generals for them. The more guard stations you have, the more generals you need.

ARMORY

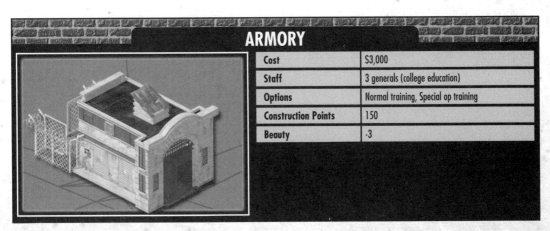

Cost	$3,000
Staff	3 generals (college education)
Options	Normal training, Special op training
Construction Points	150
Beauty	-3

You can't hire soldiers if they don't have weapons and weapons stores, and that's where the armories come in. Keep in mind that you need one general for every guard post. So, if you build six guard posts, you'll need two fully staffed armories.

As a precaution, you may want more generals than guard posts. If one happens to quit, you'll have one in reserve waiting to fill the vacancy.

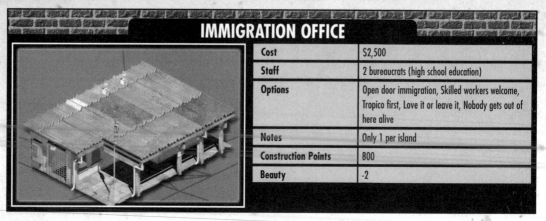

IMMIGRATION OFFICE

Cost	$2,500
Staff	2 bureaucrats (high school education)
Options	Open door immigration, Skilled workers welcome, Tropico first, Love it or leave it, Nobody gets out of here alive
Notes	Only 1 per island
Construction Points	800
Beauty	-2

Early in the game, you can increase the flow of immigrants by building an immigration office with an open-door immigration policy.

Once factories are in place, you need skilled workers so you can change the immigration office's policy to Skilled workers welcome. You may want to set this option at the start to build a reserve of educated workers.

The option Tropico first basically closes the door to immigrants, while Love it or leave it kicks out unhappy elements in your population, which can help if things start looking a little dangerous. The option Nobody gets out of here alive throws up an iron curtain so that your skilled workers can't flee should things get bad.

RADIO STATION

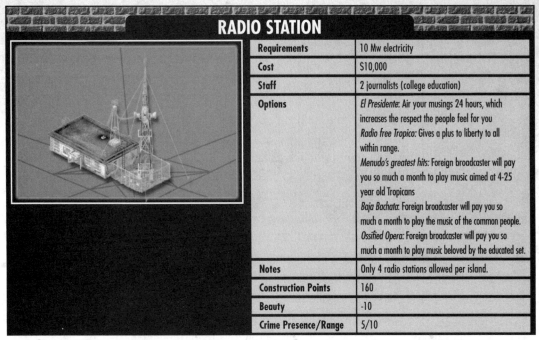

Requirements	10 Mw electricity
Cost	$10,000
Staff	2 journalists (college education)
Options	*El Presidente*: Air your musings 24 hours, which increases the respect the people feel for you *Radio free Tropico*: Gives a plus to liberty to all within range. *Menudo's greatest hits*: Foreign broadcaster will pay you so much a month to play music aimed at 4-25 year old Tropicans *Baja Bachata*: Foreign broadcaster will pay you so much a month to play the music of the common people. *Ossified Opera*: Foreign broadcaster will pay you so much a month to play music beloved by the educated set.
Notes	Only 4 radio stations allowed per island.
Construction Points	160
Beauty	-10
Crime Presence/Range	5/10

Ah, the tool of any iron-fisted tyrant, the media. Once your electricity is in place, spread the word of your enlightened rule to all that will hear, and please various factions among your people.

NEWSPAPER

Cost	$7,500
Staff	3 journalists (college education)
Options	*Voice of the workers*: +1 to +10 percent with communist faction, depending on experience of journalists. *Financial times*: +1 to +10 % with capitalists. *Soldado de fortuna*: +1 to 10% with militants. *The word of God*: +1 to 10% with religious faction. *Coupons 'n' more*: Foreign publisher will pay you so much a month per adult Tropican to print their coupons, again partly dependent on journalist experience.
Notes	4 allowed per island
Construction Points	240
Beauty	-10
Pollution/Range	5/10
Crime Presence/Range	5/10

Don't overlook the press. It can be a great tool for pleasing certain factions amongst your populace. Take note that a newspaper does *not* require electricity, but is nearly as useful to you as radio and TV stations.

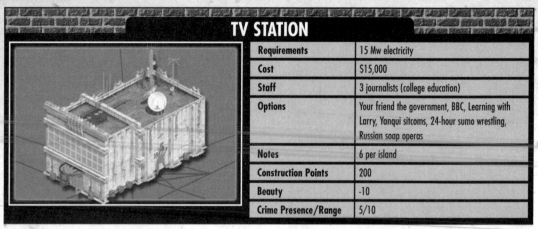

TV STATION	
Requirements	15 Mw electricity
Cost	$15,000
Staff	3 journalists (college education)
Options	Your friend the government, BBC, Learning with Larry, Yanqui sitcoms, 24-hour sumo wrestling, Russian soap operas
Notes	6 per island
Construction Points	200
Beauty	-10
Crime Presence/Range	5/10

Similar to newspapers and radio, TV stations can boost your popularity with certain factions and it can also put a little money in your pocket! Foreign broadcasters will pay you to air their shows.

Click on your TV station to see its range. Anything in green can receive your station's signal.

▷ **Your government, your friend:** Increases the love the little people have for their great leader.

▷ **BBC:** Increases the liberty your people feel.

▷ **Learning with Larry:** Doubles the rate at which your workers gain experience.

▷ **Yanqui sitcoms, Russian Soap Operas, 24 hour sumo wrestling:** Foreign broadcasters pay you so much a month (varies by experience level of your journalists) to air their programs. Sumo wrestling earns you the most, sitcoms the least.

HUMAN SERVICES

The human services on Tropico see to many of your people's needs. Sooner or later, your people will tire of snake oil medicine as an ointment and clamor for a clinic. A church is a good early investment, and don't neglect the construction of a high school. Your people do not have the education to be factory workers, and it is expensive to import them.

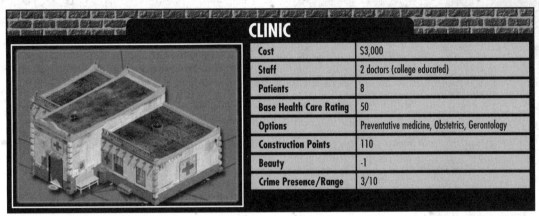

CLINIC

Cost	$3,000
Staff	2 doctors (college educated)
Patients	8
Base Health Care Rating	50
Options	Preventative medicine, Obstetrics, Gerontology
Construction Points	110
Beauty	-1
Crime Presence/Range	3/10

Clinics primarily function to provide basic health care to the populace. If you have an aging population, you'll need gerontology clinics (check the Age page in your almanac). You should definitely have a Preventative medicine clinic and an Obstetrics clinic. You should build these structures before you have a college, which means you must hire the workers from overseas. You'll need at least one in place to keep the people from grumbling about their medical care.

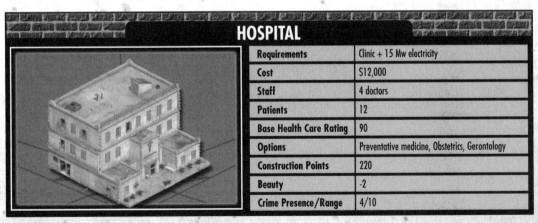

HOSPITAL

Requirements	Clinic + 15 Mw electricity
Cost	$12,000
Staff	4 doctors
Patients	12
Base Health Care Rating	90
Options	Preventative medicine, Obstetrics, Gerontology
Construction Points	220
Beauty	-2
Crime Presence/Range	4/10

A hospital can serve many more people than your clinics and once the population grows, an enlightened ruler would do well to put one in place. Of course, you can probably band-aid things along with just a string of clinics. If the people have never seen a hospital, how will they know what they're missing?

CHURCH

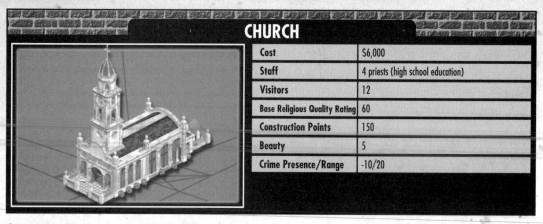

Cost	$6,000
Staff	4 priests (high school education)
Visitors	12
Base Religious Quality Rating	60
Construction Points	150
Beauty	5
Crime Presence/Range	-10/20

Sooner or later, your people will clamor for a church. Beat them to the punch and put one up early on. Make sure it is fully staffed, and hire from overseas to do so if needed. Not every high school educated male wants to be a priest; he must be religiously inclined. Priests can be difficult to find, so pay them well.

CATHEDRAL

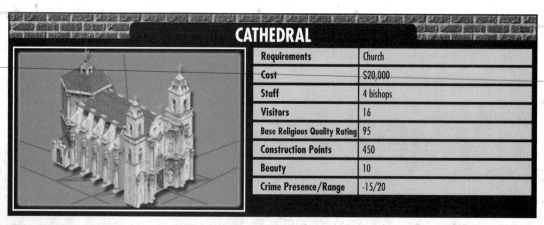

Requirements	Church
Cost	$20,000
Staff	4 bishops
Visitors	16
Base Religious Quality Rating	95
Construction Points	450
Beauty	10
Crime Presence/Range	-15/20

Do you want your workers content, el Presidente? Happy even? After building a church, you should eventually consider a cathedral and see that it's fully staffed. Religion gives the people comfort, your Excellency!

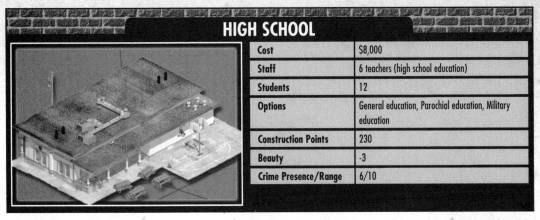

HIGH SCHOOL

Cost	$8,000
Staff	6 teachers (high school education)
Students	12
Options	General education, Parochial education, Military education
Construction Points	230
Beauty	-3
Crime Presence/Range	6/10

A high school is more than something you need to construct to keep your eggheads happy. Industries need workers with a high school education. At first, hiring them from overseas is relatively inexpensive, but the price quickly escalates. It is best to build a high school fairly early on so that you can train your own people to work in your industries. If there are more teachers than students over a period of time, fire one or two and close off the empty slots.

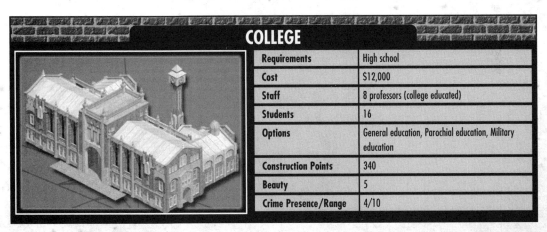

COLLEGE

Requirements	High school
Cost	$12,000
Staff	8 professors (college educated)
Students	16
Options	General education, Parochial education, Military education
Construction Points	340
Beauty	5
Crime Presence/Range	4/10

Once a high school is in place and some of your industry is up and running, you must think about electric power plants, hospitals, cathedrals and the like. Workers at those facilities need a college education, and they're even more expensive to import.

Why not build a college first and teach your own? Just make sure you have some jobs for the college educated when they finish. You should probably hire the first professor or two from overseas. Don't overstaff your colleges in later years.

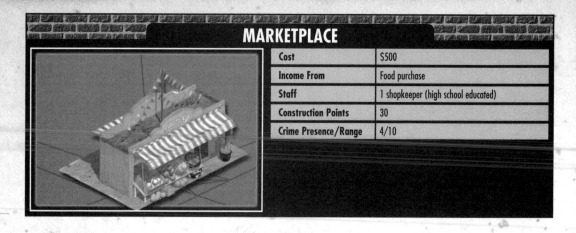

MARKETPLACE

Cost	$500
Income From	Food purchase
Staff	1 shopkeeper (high school educated)
Construction Points	30
Crime Presence/Range	4/10

Build your marketplace early and build it somewhere between where your people live and work. This helps reduce travel time and keeps them working longer. Without a marketplace, your people must walk to the farms for food. A marketplace also keeps food on hand all year round, significantly reducing the chance of food shortages.

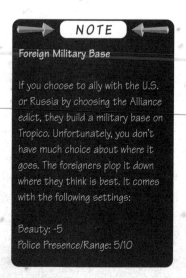

NOTE

Foreign Military Base

If you choose to ally with the U.S. or Russia by choosing the Alliance edict, they build a military base on Tropico. Unfortunately, you don't have much choice about where it goes. The foreigners plop it down where they think is best. It comes with the following settings:

Beauty: -5
Police Presence/Range: 5/10

LANDSCAPING AND ROADS

If you have much industry, you will eventually have some pollution. As mentioned earlier in this chapter, many structures have beauty ratings in the negative numbers. Landscaping is a relatively inexpensive way to beautify these places.

A few well placed statues and shrubs around your ugliest areas will go a long way toward appeasing those who worry about the environment or complain about pollution. Do not underestimate the effect of landscaping on tourists, who take much delight in seeing flowers and trees.

Try your hand at creating beautiful garden spots like this. Tropicans (and tourists!) will delight in them. "Yes, his will is iron, but he loves the people—look at the lovely flowers he plants for us."

Type	Cost	Beauty	Construction Points
Fountain	$200	9	20
Large Fountain	$1000	21	50
Statue	$600	5	25
Wild Shrub	$25 to $75	.3 to .7	N/A
Wild Tree	$50	1.0	N/A
Hedgerow	$25	.9	N/A
Ornament Bush	$75	1.2	N/A
Ornament Tree	$100	4.5	N/A
Flowers	$25	2.5	N/A

Roads are a simple matter. You do not NEED them, but they make the hauling of goods and services much faster, hence netting you more money. If nothing else, consider building them on steep grades and inclines so that your little people can get to and from their jobs more quickly.

Lastly, it is important to mention something about bulldozers. While there is an attractive little bulldozer icon on your Excellency's control screen, your worker's do not require this capitalist luxury and use their shovels to demolish what you mark. If you demolish anything, it is likely to be shacks. Remember that shacks fall apart once abandoned, but if they pop up near your luxury hotels (your people, Excellency, have they no sense?) you should get rid of them quickly.

CHAPTER 6
EDICTS: THROWING MONEY AT THE PROBLEM

"A single death is a tragedy; a million is a statistic."

—Stalin

Comrade Presidente, you should not overlook edicts. Oh, I know that they involve many papers, but if you declare what you wish you must only sign them. There is usually a fee of some sort as well, but one does not get something for nothing, eh?

There are five types of edicts:

> **People:** Edicts to use against individual Tropicans.

> **Foreign Policy:** Edicts to use to receive aid from the U.S. or Russia.

> **Economic:** Edicts that give Tropico's economy a boost.

> **Political/Religious:** Edicts that alter Tropico's political makeup.

> **Social:** Edicts that affect groups of people.

To select the choice of edicts, click on the rolled up document icon to the left of the central control panel. This takes you to a sub-menu showing you all the available edicts.

Want an edict? Click here.

> **TIP**

You can cancel some edicts. To cancel an edict, choose the edict, and then click on the cancel button in the circle window.

PEOPLE EDICTS

You probably won't use people edicts as often as the other edicts. You will more often need to influence entire groups of people rather than individuals.

The problem with edicts against people is that they don't always work. Issuing an edict against someone can actually have an effect opposite of what you intend.

Selecting a hit on someone.

To issue an edict against someone, click on the edict and then click on the individual. Have you lost sight of the person you intended to issue the edict on? Pause the game and search the building where they're employed. You may not know the exact building, but you probably know which type of building they work at. If you can't remember the name of the person but remember the political faction, access the almanac (press the A key), go to the Political page and look up factions. The person you want is likely the head of the faction.

If you don't remember the name of the person, where they worked, or what faction they were with, you won't be able to issue the edict. Always pay special attention to those who are running against you in elections (your opponent's name, job, and faction always appear when the election is announced). Always take note of which faction is having trouble with you—it is the leader of the faction who does the speaking. Keep an eye on those troublemakers, and issue an edict against them if you must. Just be warned: If there is great hostility against you, arresting one leader or killing another doesn't solve the problem. Others will soon rise against you.

So, when should you issue edicts against people? In general, when you have a large population on a well-developed island you'll have the cash and the police/soldiers/bishops to carry out the edict efficiently. Also, the negative impact on the target person and his or her family is relatively small in comparison to your overall population and mitigating dangers of a coup, uprising, bad faction rating, election loss, and so on.

ARREST

COST:	$500
DURATION:	5-year jail term
REQUIREMENTS:	Police station, Prison
EFFECTS:	Target's respect for you strongly decreases, target's family has a lesser decrease of respect toward you, and bystanders have a small decrease of respect toward you.

That's right, throw those troublemakers in jail, your Excellency! While this can work, it may not work for long. However, when used in combination with the Open the Jails edict, it can be quite useful. The Open the Jails edict is one of the political/religious edicts, discussed later in this chapter.

BRIBE

COST:	$1,000
DURATION:	Declining effect over 3 years
REQUIREMENTS:	Bank
EFFECTS:	Target's respect for you increases strongly, target family's respect for you has a lesser increase.

Bribes are more expensive than jailing or killing an opponent. On the other hand, they can turn your detractor around and influence a number of people toward you positively, at least for a few years. Sometimes you just need to buy a little time…

HERETIC

COST:	$500
DURATION:	Permanent
REQUIREMENTS:	Cathedral
EFFECTS:	Target becomes shunned by society, can't protest or lead a coup or uprising. Target and family lose respect for you.

You can destroy some poor Tropican's life with this edict, but you will make enemies in the process. Fortunately, the lack of respect from family fades over time.

ELIMINATE

COST:	$500
DURATION:	Permanent
REQUIREMENTS:	Guard tower
EFFECTS:	Strongly decrease respect for you by target's extended family and bystanders.

You desire to order a hit, your Excellency? It will be done. Why spend the money on a bribe when you can merely silence the problem?

FOREIGN POLICY EDICTS

It's possible to play a very successful and enjoyable game of Tropico without ever issuing any foreign policy edicts. Foreign policy is either pro U.S. or pro Russian, and which superpower you decide to cozy up with depends a lot upon what your game plan is. Their aid packages are very similar, except that developmental aid from the U.S. is of higher tech.

Also, better relations with the superpowers will result in more generous grants of cash from them. Direct cash foreign aid is linked to the level of your relations with the superpowers and the size of the population on the island (they're more generous if you have a larger population).

Before you can issue foreign policy edicts with the U.S. or Russia, you must have relations with them in the cold or better category. To learn where your relations stand, press the A key to access the almanac, then go to the Foreign Policy page.

Praising the United States. Praising the superpower of your choice improves relations and leads to better things.

If you plan to pursue a foreign policy game, decide before you start the game which power you want to work with. Then build your dictator accordingly, choosing attributes with lots of pluses toward either the U.S. or Russia.

Make sure you pick the diplomat option so that you can start with an embassy. If you have great relations to start with and an embassy from the get go, you can get a trade delegation or developmental aid right from the start of the game!

> *TIP*
>
> You can issue a foreign policy edict only once every two years.

If you feel especially sneaky, you can work with one superpower, and then switch to the other. It's possible to do this over the course of the game. As an example, you may wish to work with the Russians first for help getting started, and then later praising the U.S. so you can get help with the high-tech stuff. Just don't form an alliance with one if you intend to work with the other later!

There are eight foreign policy edicts, but when you reduce them to two flavors (U.S. or Russian) there are really only four kinds.

PRAISE U.S./PRAISE RUSSIA

COST:	$500
DURATION:	3 years
REQUIREMENTS:	Embassy
EFFECTS:	Increases goodwill of praised superpower, lowers goodwill of other superpower

Use this edict if you want to get the other foreign policy edicts, but your relations with the superpower you desire aid from aren't all that good. It will boost their feeling toward you, and with improved relations you should be able to get to the more lucrative foreign policy edicts.

TRADE DELEGATION TO U.S./RUSSIA

COST:	$1,000
DURATION:	Varies
REQUIREMENTS:	Relations with superpower cold or better, Airport
EFFECTS:	Variable: One-time foreign aid (cash!), higher export prices, free buildings, or free skilled workers

This is an investment that's difficult to beat! You can spend cash to get more, or other goodies.

You need to spend cash to make cash!

U.S./RUSSIAN DEVELOPMENTAL AID

COST:	$2,000
DURATION:	Permanent
REQUIREMENTS:	Relationship with superpower cool or better.
EFFECTS:	See below.

The style of developmental aid is the greatest difference between the two superpowers. The U.S. will give you plans that reduce airport and electric power plant construction costs by a whopping 50%. This is definitely the ripe banana if you plan to focus on tourism (rich tourists need an airport and a power plant to power their casinos, nightclubs, luxury hotels, and so on).

This is not an option that will come in handy early in the game, of course, since you're unlikely to require an airport or power plant at the start.

The Russians will give you plans that reduce the cost of constructing tenement and apartment complexes by 50%. This is definitely the route to take if you want to keep the workers content but not happy. You can then build cheap housing even more cheaply than usual, and spend money instead on your plantations and factories.

ALLIANCE WITH U.S./RUSSIA

COST:	$6,000
DURATION:	Permanent
REQUIREMENTS:	Very good or better relations with superpower
EFFECTS:	See below.

As mentioned previously, there's no turning back from this option, so don't choose to ally with one if you think you might want to work with the other later. After selecting an alliance, the superpower slaps an ugly military base on your island without even consulting you about where it will go. (They might put it down right next to your hotels.) Plan on landscaping around it, because it's an eyesore.

Allying with the U.S. A cruiser appears in the circle window.

The good thing is that your new ally will pay you $1,000 a year, and they'll be even better disposed toward you than ever. The bad news is that their rival will like you less. However, a super-power won't invade if you have a military base from another superpower. However, if relations with your new muchacho ever turn sour, then they might just invade. You don't want to spend your retirement years in a re-education camp in Siberia or in a federal institution, do you?

Do you really want a military base on your island?

ECONOMIC EDICTS

You'll likely issue more economic edicts than any other kind. They can have a tremendous effect on the amount of pesos in your treasury. Regardless if your intent is to make the people happy or to plan for retirement, you need money. It doesn't take a big shot to know that a good economy means mucho dinero.

Note that many of these edicts positively influence tourism. Don't issue these one-time tourism edicts until your hotels and attractions are in place, or you will waste your money. Since these are one-time only boosters (each good for three years), consider issuing each of the one-time edicts every three years.

INDUSTRY AD CAMPAIGN

COST:	$8,000
DURATION:	3 years
REQUIREMENTS:	2 factories, TV station
EFFECTS:	See below.

The price may seem high, but if you have a lot of goods leaving Tropico, this can be an immense boost. Save this one until your industry is large, since it raises the prices for exported Tropican factory goods (cigars, rum, canned goods, lumber, jewelry) by 20%!

AIR POLLUTION STANDARDS

COST:	$500
DURATION:	Permanent
REQUIREMENTS:	Any factory
EFFECTS:	See below.

Factories are polluters. If your people grow more and more upset about the smog, issue this edict to reduce pollution by 50%! Unfortunately, factory maintenance cost will climb 20%.

When you pass the pollution edict, the black smoke stops pouring out of the factory smokestacks.

If you have lots of cash pouring in, you might not even notice the difference, but if things are tight, this could break you. Fortunately, you can always reverse this edict if need be.

TOURISM AD CAMPAIGN

COST:	$5,000
DURATION:	3 years
REQUIREMENTS:	Any hotel, TV station
EFFECTS:	See below.

Do you have any hotels? Do you have lots of attractions for your tourists to see? Is pollution down? Crime under control? Then issue this edict. It will bring in the tourists and they will pay even higher room rates than normal.

THE HEADLINER

COST:	$5,000
DURATION:	3 years
REQUIREMENTS:	Nightclub
EFFECTS:	See below.

Like the tourism ad campaign, this is wasted money unless the tourism industry is flourishing or starting to flourish. Upon launching this edict, an aging but popular singer comes to Tropico. Tourism ratings climb 20%, but your little people love the singer too, and they flock to see him, raising entertainment quality for Tropicans 10%. U.S. relations even improve 10%, so this is a good thing all around.

TAX CUT

COST:	$200 per adult islander
DURATION:	3 years
REQUIREMENTS:	None
EFFECTS:	See below.

This is a great edict to issue if your respect is taking a nosedive in the ratings, provided you have the extra cash, especially if an election is coming up. In fact, it's a good idea to keep a cash reserve around so you can issue this edict at election time. Combined with across the board pay raises, you can squeeze out of many an election jam this way.

Giving the money to the people—but look at your treasury numbers sink.

SPECIAL BUILDING PERMIT

COST:	$500
DURATION:	Permanent
REQUIREMENTS:	None
EFFECTS:	See below.

If you want to earn the pesos, this is the edict for you. All construction costs will increase by 20%, which is bad, but 10% of that number will go into your Swiss bank account, which is very good, no? The eggheads will discover the $200 dollar hammers and screwdrivers on your building invoices and figure out what you're up to, thus lowering your standing with them by 10%.

Still, as every Presidente needs to build and every Presidente needs some extra pesos, so this is a very useful edict indeed. Note that you can always cancel it if needed to boost your standing with the intellectuals or save a little money. Note that for a $1000 building, this edict raises the cost by $200, of which $100 goes into your Swiss bank account. In effect, you're converting money from your treasury to your Swiss bank account at a 2 to 1 ratio.

PAN-CARIBBEAN GAMES

COST:	$7,500
DURATION:	3 years
REQUIREMENTS:	Sports complex
EFFECTS:	See below.

This is another great boost for your island's tourist trade. Hosting the Pan-Caribbean games increases your tourist rating by 50%, and the little people's entertainment value by 20%. Unfortunately, you can only host the games once.

MARDI GRAS

COST:	$3,000
DURATION:	3 years
REQUIREMENTS:	Pub
EFFECTS:	See below.

Here is the edict you're likely to issue more often than any other. There is no faster way to improve the mood of your people, which as you no doubt know, your Excellency, is sometimes necessary just prior to elections. Some past leaders have enacted this edict as often as possible, because they cared for the happiness of their people.

Let the entertainment commence when you issue the Mardi Gras edict.

Issuing this edict increases the tourism rating by 20%, improves the local entertainment quality by 30% (and quickly!), but increases crime by 20%. (With everyone staggering drunk, it is much easier to pick their pockets.)

The Mardi Gras edict is one of your best tools for pleasing Tropicans.

POLITICAL AND RELIGIOUS EDICTS

Most political and religious edicts are considered repressive by the unenlightened. You will no doubt find them useful for maintaining order.

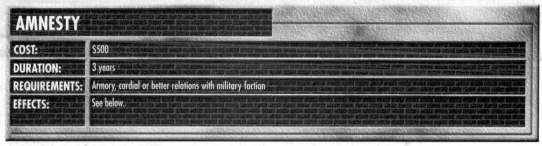

AMNESTY

COST:	$500
DURATION:	3 years
REQUIREMENTS:	Armory, cordial or better relations with military faction
EFFECTS:	See below.

If you encounter trouble from the rebels, you may not have to fight them. You can win them over instead. The problem is that you must have improved the overall happiness on Tropico by at least 5% since any given rebel became a rebel for him or her to consider accepting your offer. In fact, you're more likely to convert rebels back to normal society if happiness has improved by 10% or more. With Amnesty in effect, rebels are four times more likely to revert to society than normal.

If you have a serious rebel problem, consider using various tools (tax cuts, pay raises, Mardi Gras, etc.) to boost overall happiness, and then issue the Amnesty edict.

EARLY ELECTION

COST:	$2,000
DURATION:	Instant
REQUIREMENTS:	None
EFFECTS:	See below.

If things are going well but you have plans that might shift public opinion (perhaps the little people do not understand your grand vision), this is a great option.

You can hold elections while things are in your favor, and then do whatever needs to be done without the worry of rigging an election or even canceling it. Once issued, an election will occur in one year's time. You can only issue this edict once every three years.

INQUISITION

COST:	$500
DURATION:	Permanent
REQUIREMENTS:	Cathedral, cordial or better relations with religious faction
EFFECTS:	See below.

This is one of several edicts that tighten your grip on the people, your Excellency. An inquisition significantly reduces the chance of protests or uprisings, and slightly reduces the chance for a coup. It does slightly increase the chance for rebel activity, decreases the people's liberty score by 25%, and lowers tourism by 25%. However, it does double church attendance! You can cancel this edict at any time.

Let heretics and infidels beware!
The inquisition has begun.

BOOK BBQ

COST:	$500
DURATION:	Permanent
REQUIREMENTS:	Church, Cool or better relations with the religious faction
EFFECTS:	See below.

If the eggheads have been stirring up trouble, this edict reduces the size of their numbers by 50%! Unfortunately, without any intellectuals, there will be no one to teach your people and education rates also drop 50%. This isn't a good edict to issue when you're trying to educate Tropicans for factory jobs. You can cancel this edict at any time.

MARTIAL LAW

COST:	$5,000
DURATION:	Permanent
REQUIREMENTS:	Cordial or better relations with the military faction
EFFECTS:	See below.

Although this edict has no effect on coups or rebels, it greatly reduces the chance of protests or uprisings and decreases the crime rate by 40%. It also decreases productivity by 20%. (A fearful worker is an unproductive worker, el Presidente!)

If you are concerned with liberty, you will be saddened to learn that this edict decreases it by 50%. This edict also lowers tourism by 50%. But if you need to use this edict, you're probably setting up Tropico as a vast plantation or industrial park, and the tourism effect won't hurt you. You can cancel this edict at any time.

The best use for Martial Law occurs when you're in good standing with the army, but the population is angry with you. Issue this edict, ignore elections, and keep the soldiers loyal.

OPEN THE JAILS

COST:	$3,000
DURATION:	Instant
REQUIREMENTS:	Prison
EFFECTS:	See below.

If you previously used the arrest edict to cram the jails full of your opponents, you can dispose of them for good and not cause an uproar about bloodshed. That's right, just open your jails. This expels all of the inmates from the island! U.S. goodwill will lower by 10%, but who cares what the meddling yanquis think, eh?

PAPAL VISIT

COST:	$10,000
DURATION:	3 years
REQUIREMENTS:	Cathedral, Cordial or better relations with religious faction
EFFECTS:	See below.

Everyone on Tropico loves the Pope, even the communists. If you can afford his visit, respect for you in the eyes of the religious faction will rise 50% and all other factions will respect you 15% more. Total religious happiness will rise 25%. Unfortunately, the Pope is very busy, and can only visit Tropico once.

This is a very useful edict if you need a respect boost, or if you're close to achieving happiness for your people but just can't quite get the religion score up where it needs to be. A visit from the Pope will work, well, miracles!

Having the Pope visit is a boost to many of your popularity figures.

SOCIAL EDICTS

Social edicts impact how your people behave. Your word is law, and you can impact the future of the entire island by enacting any of these edicts. Naturally, some are more useful than others are.

PROHIBITION	
COST:	$500
DURATION:	Permanent
REQUIREMENTS:	None
EFFECTS:	See below.

This edict bans alcohol from Tropico and, as a result, the crime rate skyrockets by 100%. This edict forces all pubs and nightclubs to close (not to mention rum distilleries).

The edict does increase your respect among the religious population by 10%, and increases worker productivity by 10%. You may want to use it to give Tropico an industrial boost, or if you want to curry favor with the religious faction. Fortunately, you can cancel the edict at any time.

Use this edict if you plan to ignore tourism and if you have a character trait (like Chief of Police) that counteracts the increased crime. Don't build any pubs and issue this edict early to take full advantage of the productivity boost.

LITERACY PROGRAM

COST:	$500
DURATION:	Permanent
REQUIREMENTS:	High School
EFFECTS:	See below.

This is one of the most useful edicts you can issue. I'm sure you are tired of hearing it by now, el Presidente, but the better educated your people are, the more qualified they are to work in your factories, nightclubs, and casinos. Hiring local labor is far cheaper than overseas labor.

Give your Tropicans educational support.

Choosing this edict means that workers and students learn 30% faster (meaning they get educated more quickly, and get more experienced faster). Literacy is not free, though; in addition to the initial $500 price tag, this edict costs $2 per Tropican annually to maintain. Still, that price isn't much considering the benefit it brings. You can cancel this edict at any time.

You may want to issue this edict early in the game, when your workers are unskilled to increase their skills. Then after about 5 years, cancel it when their skills level off.

CONTRACEPTION BAN

COST:	$500
DURATION:	Permanent
REQUIREMENTS:	Church, Cool or better relations with the religious faction
EFFECTS:	See below.

If you don't have enough immigrants coming in but need some labor, this will net you some home-grown workers. It increases your standing with the religious faction by 10%, so it's effective at winning their favor. It also boosts the population growth by 30%, but decreases respect of the intellectuals by 30%. You can cancel this edict at any time.

ANTI-LITTER ORDINANCE

COST:	$500
DURATION:	Permanent
REQUIREMENTS:	None
EFFECTS:	See below.

If you want to make Tropico truly sparkle and have already cut down on pollution and added beautiful landscaping, consider the anti-litter ordinance. This edict reduces pollution by individuals by 50%, and decreases Tropican liberty by 10%. Note that this edict does not reduce industrial pollution. You can cancel this edict at any time.

SENSITIVITY TRAINING

COST:	$500
DURATION:	Permanent
REQUIREMENTS:	College
EFFECTS:	See below.

El Presidente, the people do not always care for your policemen and soldiers. Some find them… threatening. This edict provides classes for your enforcers so that they are more sensitive to the people's feelings, and reduces ill will toward them by 50%.

Help your policemen and soldiers learn sensitivity.

This edict costs $50 dollars per soldier and policeman (per year) to maintain. You can cancel it at any time.

FOOD FOR THE PEOPLE

COST:	$500
DURATION:	Permanent
REQUIREMENTS:	None
EFFECTS:	See below.

Issuing this edict improves the food quality rating of a fully fed citizen from 70 to 100, which boosts overall satisfaction with your regime. However, you must be careful, because the edict also doubles food consumption. Before issuing it, determine the number of people on Tropico (the population appears in the lower-right corner of your screen, under the circle window) and then count the number of farms.

Remember, a fully staffed farm (or wharf) feeds 30-40 people. If you have 200 people, you'll need 5 farms normally, so in this example you would need 10 farms for this edict. You must also watch your population carefully. Remember that farms growing coffee, sugar, or tobacco don't produce food crops, so don't work them into your calculations! You can cancel this edict at any time.

CHAPTER 7

VICTORY STRATEGIES

"But men generally decide upon a middle course, which is most hazardous, for they know neither how to be entirely good nor entirely bad."
—*Machiavelli*

Of course you wish your rule to be a great one, el Presidente! But what one might call great, another, well, would be less satisfied with. A great victory for one is a loss for another. How you play Tropico will naturally depend upon what victory conditions you choose (or pre-exist, in the case of the pre-designed scenarios) as well as your own style of play.

Regardless, there are some things every good Presidente must know.

GAME INTERFACE

The more familiar you are with the game interface, the better you will know how to manage Tropico. Play through the tutorial before you play your first game, and then play it again later—you might notice something you didn't the first time through.

VIEWING TROPICO

By clicking on the + or − keys in the map area on the bottom-left of the screen, you can zoom far above the island or close in on buildings or individuals. The arrows on the map area enable you to rotate your view so that you can get a better look at something that might be hidden from one angle.

The + or - keys and the rotate arrows are located in the bottom-left corner.

THE CENTRAL CONTROL PANEL

The building, edict, and info mode are discussed throughout this book. In summary, to access building options, click on the hammer icon, to select edicts, click on the rolled-up paper icon, and to monitor the island and obtain information, click on the icon of the open eye.

THE CIRCLE WINDOW

The circle window is on the bottom-right side of the screen. This window displays different things at different times. For example, when you select an edict, it displays an animation of the edict taking effect. When you click on an individual Tropican, the circle window zooms in on them.

The circle window shows a close-up of whatever you clicked on most recently, in this case, a cigar factory.

SPEED CONTROL

Beneath the circle window are the all-important speed control bars. You can adjust the speed of the game from pause to very fast by clicking on the bar of your choice (pause is the smallest option, on the left).

Although you may want to play the first few years on fast speed, a fast game speed can be a real detriment to good gameplay. You may want to keep it on slow so that you can monitor all of the factors that keep Tropico working much more easily.

If you want to make a number of changes or just look things over prior to an election, you should pause the game. By pausing the game, the months don't slip by while no orders are being issued. Just don't forget to restart the game!

ISLAND STATS PANEL

There are four boxes and a meter just below the speed control that you should definitely keep an eye on. The four boxes, from left to right, top then bottom, are:

▷ **Treasury:** The amount of money in Tropico's treasury (clicking it calls up the Economics page of the almanac).

- ▷ **Date:** You guessed it, el Presidente, the current month and year (clicking it brings up the Overview page of the almanac).

- ▷ **Swiss Bank Account:** The amount of money you've socked away for retirement (clicking it calls up the Overview page of the almanac).

- ▷ **Population:** The number of Tropicans on your island (clicking it accesses the Lists page of the almanac).

Beneath these four boxes is a little meter indicating the overall happiness for all Tropicans (clicking it accesses the Happiness page of the almanac).

OPTIONS

Clicking the little open book to the left side of the circle brings up seven more buttons that enable you to load a map, save a map, take you back to the main game menu, quit, cancel and return to the game, and change the settings. You may want to change the settings if the game is running a little slow (you can decrease the finesse of the graphics).

Save often, your Excellency!

You should definitely make frequent use of the save map function, regardless of your game style or victory conditions! Allow me to suggest, your Excellency, that you always save before a big expenditure or election. In case something goes wrong, you can try again.

THE ALMANAC

Excellency, if you have read other sections of the book you have doubtless heard much of the almanac already. Without repeating myself or boring you, let me just say how useful the almanac is and how often you should use it to monitor the island. It comes up automatically at the end of every year, but you can access it at any time by pressing the A key.

The Government Stability page, accessed from the Politics page of the almanac.

Past Tropican rulers have not made good use of the almanac, and where are they today? Forgotten. Do not make the same mistake! Familiarize yourself with the pages of the almanac, and learn how to put them to use. (Other sections of the book discuss how to use it for specific purposes.)

STARTING UP

The game has begun. Before you do anything else, pause the game. Now zoom out and press the info icon (the eye) and click on the overall icon (the little island). Cycle through the crops to see which grow best where, and cycle through your minerals (if you have any) to see what kind they are, and where they are located. It goes without saying that if you see a rich deposit of gold, you should not build an apartment over it.

Looking at a corn farm.

While the game is paused, switch some of your farms to tobacco (or another cash producing crop, like coffee or pineapple, depending on what the soil conditions are). How many farms you switch depends upon your population. You need to have enough farms producing food that you can feed about twice your starting population, because it will grow fast and you need a safety buffer.

Now go the presidential palace and raise the salary of your guard to $12. Over the course of the first decade, gradually increase soldier pay to $15-16. Now it is time to build.

FIRST BUILDINGS

While the game is still paused, consider your next options carefully. You should always address housing next, because your people despise living in shacks. Remember not to build on some of the best tobacco land or over a gold mine, as mentioned in the previous section.

If you started as a diplomat and have cool or better relations with the Russians, sign up right away for developmental aid so that you can get apartments at half cost. If you don't have an agreement with the Russians, put up a tenement right away. The sooner you can get people into housing, the better.

With the ministry in place, you can issue foreign policy edicts.

The next thing you should build is another construction office so that you can work faster.

Finally, you'll need additional income because two tobacco farms are not enough to generate the cash you'll need. You basically have three options: a mine, a logging camp, or a few more farms. If there is a good gold deposit nearby, definitely build a mine. If there is bauxite, a mine is probably worthwhile; if there is iron or no strong deposits nearby, hold off on mining for the time being.

Just after the game begins, look at the over-all minerals. In this figure, there is a huge mineral deposit right next to some farms.

If mining isn't feasible, look at soil conditions for a good cash crop. Tobacco and sugar are best, but coffee and pineapples also work.

TIP

Never be afraid to bulldoze. That's right, you can bulldoze buildings. It is especially important to bulldoze obsolete structures—a logging camp that is now in the middle of your city because you've had to expand out around it. Simply click the bulldozing icon on the struc- ture, and it will be marked for destruction. Make sure you build additional housing before demolish- ing any current housing. The people will be very angry if you destroy their homes and give them nowhere to go.

Finally, if there is a dense forest nearby and you don't plan to build regular buildings in the forest soon, construct a logging camp or two.

Regardless, build at least one or two more income producers early in order to pay for the social infrastructure you'll soon need.

At about the 5-year mark, you should have some nice profits rolling in. Build the following in this order: a pub, a church, and a clinic (you'll probably need to hire some foreign skilled workers for the latter two). Then build a high school to start training the large numbers of skilled workers you'll need for later in the game.

An immigration office is very nice for luring skilled workers, lowering the population influx, getting rid of those who dislike you, or keeping everyone in. Get one, staff it well, and use it as needed.

If you plan on developing tourism, then get started immediately and construct an electrical plant. Get a school up in the first 10 years or so, and don't wait too long for the electrical plant regardless—no later than '65.

VICTORY CONDITIONS

The victory conditions are another factor in deciding the order in which to do things.

A PLACE IN HISTORY

You need to plan on doing a little bit of everything with this victory condition. Continue to build things to please the islanders and keep them reasonably content by providing good wages, housing, food, and entertainment. Consider some tourism as well as industry.

Fail to plan well, and you'll end up in a rowboat and a few hundreds...

DON'T WORRY, BE HAPPY

To keep your people happy, it is also necessary to run a balanced island because you need money to keep them happy. Try to build your cash reserves at the start and continue to issue the Mardi Gras edict.

Attempt to build up the treasury, and then two years before the end of the game, increase everyone's salary to 50. Then issue the Tax Cut edict, the Headliner edict, and any other edicts you can think of to raise your acclaim.

'TIS MONEY THAT MAKES THE MAN

For this victory condition, you don't have to be quite as balanced, although you need to appease your workers at least enough to stay in power.

Issue the Special Building Permit edict relatively early, and get lots of banks (4 or 5). Start them on Urban Development so you can build your economy cheaply, and then switch them to Swiss Banking at about the 20 or 30 year mark. You're likely to encounter more problems from the people with this approach, especially toward the end of the scenario, so don't be afraid of the harsher edicts, but don't forget the universally useful Mardi Gras edict.

ECONOMIC POWERHOUSE

Keeping your people content or happy certainly makes making money easier, so always keep that in mind. What kind of economic powerhouse you build really depends upon your island and your tastes.

Determine your island's type of natural resources, their proximity to your population centers, and your personal tastes. Do you feel more like heavy industry this time around, or do you want to build a tourist's paradise? Pick one area and specialize.

OPEN-ENDED

Because you are the judge of your performance with this victory condition, your Excellency, it is impossible to suggest any strategies here other than to choose those that you will enjoy the most.

PLAYING WITH AN IRON FIST

As mentioned previously, the best way to achieve almost any victory condition is to treat the people well. But it is possible to take another route favored by rulers throughout history, and that is to play as a ruthless dictator.

Your soldiers love the cabarets.

Before you rub your hands together with glee, el Presidente, I should point out that Niccolo Machiavelli himself recognized that dictatorship was not ideal for the long-term welfare of the state. He did write *The Prince*, full of much wisdom for those intending to dominate their people, but it was intended only as a guide book for those who wished to rule alone. He thought that dictatorship was actually poisonous for the long term welfare of a country—I refer you to his overlooked *Discourses*, full of much wisdom for republics... Your eyes glaze, el Presidente. You would rather I tell you how to crush all who oppose you, eh?

Start by choosing a character well suited for the lifestyle. A good choice is Generalissimo, Military Coup, Empathy, and Charismatic. Stay on very good terms with your military. Boost up their pay and then build houses and luxury homes that only they can afford. You can do this by raising the rent on the structures where you want them to live (remember that a Tropican can only afford a home that is one-third their combined salary).

Build cabarets, favored by the soldiers. (Review the information provided about rebels and uprisings in the "Managing Your Island" chapter.) Get the newspaper up and running as a propaganda machine, and as soon as you have electricity, get some radios and newspapers going to spread propaganda as well.

Don't forget how well bribery can work on leaders. You can also jail your most vocal opponents. Upon accumulating a number of them, you can issue the one-time Empty The Jails edict, which exiles them all from Tropico.

SCORING

Your raw score is modified by the difficulty rating of the game. Therefore, you must score twice as many points for the same final score if your difficulty rating is 50% instead of 100%.

If you're shooting for a monster score, consider accepting a number of unfavorable starting conditions that will boost the difficulty rating, but that you can dodge by effective gameplay. For example, a smaller island will boost your difficulty rating but if you use fishing wharves instead of corn farms to feed your people, you don't need as much land. If you don't plan on any mining, set mineral density to the lowest level. If you're pursuing a militarist strategy, choose Rebel Yell—your soldiers will kill the rebels any way.

Don't count on a high score if the rebels blow up your palace...

COMPETITIVE SCORING

If you want to compete with another Presidente, agree on victory conditions, dictator attributes, and island characteristics, and generate a map. Save the game right at the start, and then use the same map without employing any cheats.

Naturally, another way to compete is to play the pre-designed scenarios to see who scores higher.

C H A P T E R   8
PRE-DESIGNED SCENARIOS

"No man who ever held the office of president would congratulate a friend on obtaining it."

—John Adams

Eight pre-generated scenarios, complete with victory conditions and dictators, have been designed for your Excellency's pleasure.

To play a pre-designed scenario, click on the picture of the open book on the hand-made tapestry hanging in el Presidente's office. You will immediately see a list of choices.

I humbly offer the following suggestions for solving these scenarios. Each scenario is briefly described, and then a description of its ruler and conditions are given, along with the all-important victory tips. Viva el Presidente!

BORN AGAIN

Scenario Description: An earthquake has leveled everything except the dock, the construction office, and your magnificent palace. You do have some roads, but you have only twenty people and no farms. By the scenario's end, you must have a population of 300+, with a happiness rating of 60+. No wonder this scenario is rated very hard!

There's little left but the palace and mounds of rubble.

SCENARIO BREAKDOWN

- ▷ **Dictator characteristics:** Biblical scholar, Religious appointment, Empathy, Ugly, Religious zealot
- ▷ **Democracy expectations:** Somewhat low
- ▷ **Overall respect:** +5%
- ▷ **Religious faction:** +40%
- ▷ **Intellectual faction:** -20%
- ▷ **Tourism rating:** -10%
- ▷ **Crime rate:** -45%
- ▷ **Education:** +10%
- ▷ **Religious buildings cost:** -25%
- ▷ **Swiss banking prohibited**
- ▷ **Residents visit churches 50% more often**

SCENARIO STRATEGY

You must have a teamster office, so build one soon, but allow only 2 or 3 workers at first. Next, create some income with pineapple or tobacco farms or a logging camp. Your people need housing, and you don't have time to construct a tenement or apartment complex. Construct 5 or 6 bunkhouses, but don't delay—your people will grow angry without housing. Build one corn farm too.

Consider a diplomatic ministry near the beginning of the game to receive Russian developmental aid and get housing at half cost. To help attract people, build an immigration office and set it for open immigration. Passing a ban on contraception always helps boost population too, as does specializing your clinics and hospitals for obstetrics. Don't miss out on the gold mine on the north end of the fissure—it's mineral rich.

Invest in a church and a pub. Because immigration is slow, a church enables you to pass a contraception ban and boost population the old fashioned way. Building a pub not only helps you keep the people content, it enables you to pass the Mardi Gras edict, which you should do often.

As the population increases, build banana and papaya farms for money and food and erect fishing wharves for food as the game continues. A coffee farm or two isn't a bad idea either.

Because happiness is crucial in this scenario, use every trick up your sleeve. For example, the Tax Cut edict is a good option.

If you're still short on people near the end of the scenario, build some construction offices, which always attract workers and boost everyone's pay to pad your happiness near the end of the game.

FRUITAS

Scenario Description: Fruitas, the worldwide fruit conglomerate, bought the election for you. Now you must give them what they want, which is a lot of fruit at cut-rate costs.

You must ship them immense amounts of bananas, pineapples, and papayas, or you might wind up missing like the last el Presidente. This scenario is rated hard. The scenario ends as soon as you have shipped out 100 bananas, 100 papayas, and 100 pineapples.

SCENARIO BREAKDOWN

▷ **Dictator Characteristics:** Pop singer, Capitalist Rebellion, Charismatic, Empathy, Womanizer, The great schmoozola

▷ **Democracy expectations:** Low

▷ **Overall respect:** +20%

▷ **Religious faction:** -20%

▷ **Capitalist faction:** +10%

▷ **Intellectual faction:** -30%

▷ **Relations with USA:** +25%

▷ **Relations with Russia:** -10%

- ▷ **Liberty:** -10%

- ▷ **Tourism rating:** +10%

- ▷ **Factory productivity:** +10%

- ▷ **Nightclub rating:** +50%

- ▷ **Radio & TV dogma:** +50%

- ▷ **Respect of all women:** -10%

- ▷ **Respect of the least intelligent:** +10%

At the start of the game you receive a note from your sponsors warning you to hold up your end of the bargain.

SCENARIO STRATEGY

You start the scenario with only four farms, a cannery, a construction office, a dock, and your lovely palace. Remember that the victory conditions are only dependent on surviving long enough to deliver the fruit. Pay low and get the farms built, and construct only tenements and an occasional country house.

Make sure you build fishing piers and corn farms so that your people don't eat all of your profits. Since fruitas pay so poorly, build some mines to generate pesos so that you can keep building new farms.

Oh, and you should pay your soldiers well, el Presidente. Look into providing good housing for them too. They should be made comfortable.

ISLA DE FORESTA

Scenario Description: Tropico's forests are leveled and the economy is non-existent. You must find a new source of income. To succeed you need only last fifty years and end up with a good Swiss bank account and a good number of buildings. This scenario is rated as moderately difficult.

SCENARIO BREAKDOWN

▷ **Dictator Characteristics:** Professor, Elected as socialist, Green thumb, Scholarly, Ugly, Coward

▷ **Democracy expectations:** High

▷ **Overall respect:** -5%

▷ **Militarist faction:** -5%

▷ **Communist faction:** +10%

▷ **Intellectual faction:** +40%

▷ **Environmentalist faction:** +10%

▷ **Relations with Russia:** +15%

▷ **Liberty:** +20%

▷ **Tourism:** -10%

▷ **Factory productivity:** -10%

▷ **Pollution:** -50%

▷ **Education:** +80%

▷ **Soldiers and supporters twice as likely to flee in battle**

SCENARIO STRATEGY

You start with five logging camps, a lumber mill, a construction office, a teamster's office, one dock, four farms, some bunkhouses, and a palace.

Close down all of the logging camps, but only bulldoze the one near the closest gold mine. Plan on mining this area, soon—there's mucho gold in that vein. The other veins on the island are lucrative too, so build over them as well.

Your predecessor didn't leave many trees on Tropico.

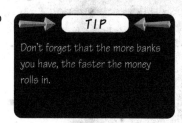

TIP

Don't forget that the more banks you have, the faster the money rolls in.

About halfway through the game, turn on the closest logging camp and the lumber mill, and then about three-quarters of the way through the game you can re-activate the far-right logging camp.

Otherwise, don't oppress your people too much—just play it safe and the money will roll in.

LOS EXCONVICTOS

Scenario Description: The oppressors have departed, leaving the inmates of their former prison colony free. There is little rain, thus meaning fewer crops, and immigrants are sparse because of the island's reputation. After 40 years, you must have fifty thousand in your coffers and 200+ people. This scenario is rated as moderately difficult.

The imperialists left their prisons behind, along with a good road system.

SCENARIO BREAKDOWN

▷ **Dictator Characteristics:** Self-made man, Elected for family values, Green thumb, Scholarly, Womanizer, Compulsive gambler

▷ **Democracy expectations:** Very high

▷ **Religious faction:** -5%

▷ **Capitalist faction:** +20%

▷ **Intellectual faction:** +20%

▷ **Environmentalist faction:** +10%

▷ **Relations with USA:** +10%

▷ **Liberty:** +20%

▷ **Tourism rating:** +10%

▷ **Factory productivity:** +5%

▷ **Pollution:** -50%

▷ **Education:** +30%

▷ **Respect of all women:** -10%

▷ **Annual gambling binge:** ($300-$1500)

SCENARIO STRATEGY

When the scenario begins, you have only a dock, two farms, a construction office, a teamster office, one police station, two prisons, and a palace.

While it is possible to win by crafting a tourist's paradise, mining may be an easier way to victory. Immediately build an iron mine near the prison, or a bauxite mine near the archeological site. Don't chase the gold deposit on the far side of the island; it's too difficult to reach and will only slow you down. Then construct housing and farms (or wharves) as needed for food. An immigration office can help lure in the workers you want. Also note that there are more eggheads than usual on the island, so building a high school early will keep them happy.

Mining is the key to this scenario—take whatever steps possible to get it rolling. Putting up construction offices will help you get more people to the island.

MI CORAZON

Scenario Description: The good news is that you're el Presidente! Congratulations! The bad news is that there will be mandatory, fair elections every few years because the world is watching. Some good can come from this, though; the U.N. will instantly build the first three buildings you choose for free. Oh, and did I mention that there is only $5,000 in the treasury? No wonder this scenario is rated so ridiculously hard. You must stay in power for 30 years, but the score is based only upon the happiness of your people.

People on this island are particularly restless. You can lose elections even with a relatively high happiness rating. Use every happiness boosting trick up your sleeve to win tight elections (pay raises, tax cuts, Mardi Gras edict, etc).

SCENARIO BREAKDOWN

- **Dictator characteristics:** Leftist author, Elected for family values, Scholarly, Coward, Cheapskate

- **Democracy expectations:** Very high

- **Overall respect:** +5%

- **Militarist faction:** -5%

- **Religious faction:** +15%

- **Intellectual faction:** +35%

- **Liberty:** +20%

- **Tourism rating:** +10%

- **Education:** +50%

- **Building costs:** -5%

- **Radio & TV dogma:** +50%

- **Soldiers and supporters twice as likely to flee in battle.**

- **Cannot pay any workers more than $25 a month.**

Before you place a free factory building, check the prevailing wind.

SCENARIO STRATEGY

When the scenario begins, you have a fisherman's wharf, a dock, one teamster's office, one construction office, five farms, four houses, a logging camp, and a palace.

The most important thing is to choose the first three buildings wisely. Choose a foreign ministry so you can get aid from the U.S. or Russians, and then build a high school and a cigar factory. Convert three farms to tobacco and build many more. Get developmental aid from the Russians and get those tenements and apartments built. Build a pub early on and issue the Mardi Gras edict as soon as possible.

NEW HAVANA

Scenario Description: When all's said and done, the objective in this scenario is to cram your Swiss bank account until it bursts. You have 50 years to get $100,000 or more into your Swiss bank account. This scenario is rated hard.

SCENARIO BREAKDOWN

▷ **Dictator Characteristics:** Self-made man, Bought the election, Charismatic, Empathy, Compulsive liar, Short tempered

▷ **Democracy expectations:** Somewhat low

▷ **Overall respect:** +15%

▷ **Militarist faction:** -10%

▷ **Religious faction:** -15%

▷ **Capitalist faction:** +10%

▷ **Intellectual faction:** -45%

▷ **Relations with USA:** +10%

▷ **Factory productivity:** +15%

▷ **Radio and TV dogma:** +50%

▷ **Can commit greater election frauds with lower consequences**

SCENARIO STRATEGY

You start this scenario with an airport, a dock, one teamster's office, a construction office, a bank, four bungalows, three farms, and a palace. The bank is already manned by two fat cats, but the airport has no workers.

This scenario seems even more difficult than it's rated. It is difficult to get all that money in on time and keep the people from throwing you into the ocean.

Switch from slush fund to urban funding.

Start with the bank on Urban Development so you can build your island more cheaply. After a few years, switch the first bank to Slush Fund and then issue the Special Building Permit edict. Make sure you have at least three banks up and running by the end of 40 years (preferably 30). You should set the other banks for your Swiss bank account.

Take advantage of the bauxite deposits and mine them for all they're worth. Build farms that produce cash crops, not just food—use fishing to feed your people.

It's crucial to remember that only your treasury must be in the black (above $0) for the banks' Slush Fund option to work, so you must keep the economy moving. Get a strong start so the treasury doesn't die early.

The final 10 years of your regime will be the worst, because it will grow more and more difficult to siphon the money you need while keeping the people content. Keep those soldiers well paid, and invest in some guard towers.

Near the end of your term, if you have issued the Special Building Permit edict, construct a lot of buildings. It doesn't matter if they get finished or not; the moment you order them built, you receive the money for them. An especially sneaky trick is to build things and then immediately cancel construction. You'll receive half of your money back, but you get to keep the full amount of the associated bribe. This is still less efficient than using banks and Slush Funds, but if you're desperate, use it.

PLANTATION PARADISE

Scenario Description: Tropico's plantation owner is dead and you have been declared their new leader. Your job is to build a good economy and make some money for yourself. You must last 50 years and boost the treasury and your Swiss bank account. The difficulty rating is hard.

SCENARIO BREAKDOWN

- **Dictator characteristics:** Man of the people, Communist rebellion, Hardworking, Entrepreneurial, Compulsive liar, Tourette's syndrome

- **Democracy expectations:** Very low

- **Overall respect:** -5%

- **Religious faction:** -20%

- **Communist faction:** +30%

- **Intellectual faction:** -15%

- **Relations with USA:** -15%

- **Relations with Russia:** +10%

- **Liberty:** -10%

- **Overall productivity:** +10%

- **Farmer productivity:** +10%

- **Overall export prices:** +10%

- **Annual pay-per-view revenue:** $1,000

SCENARIO STRATEGY

When this scenario begins, you have a diplomatic ministry, a rum distillery, a few bunkhouses, one teamster's office, a construction office, three farms, a dock, an airport, and a palace.

This scenario is much easier than it's rated. Take advantage of the mineral deposits throughout the island, and construct some mines. See if you can score in excess of 2000!

The luxurious gardens outside your palace.

THE MOTHER OF ALL CIGARS

Scenario Description: The communists took over your former island home, and your objective is to exact revenge upon them. You have 50 years to make two million dollars from El Tropicano, the world's finest cigars. The difficulty rating is hard.

SCENARIO BREAKDOWN

▷ **Dictator Characteristics:** Harvard U, Elected as capitalist, Hardworking, Financial genius, Womanizer, Alcoholic

▷ **Democracy expectations:** Very high

▷ **Religious faction:** -25%

▷ **Capitalist faction:** +25%

▷ **Relations with USA:** +45%

▷ **Relations with Russia:** -5%

▷ **Liberty:** +20%

▷ **Overall productivity:** +5%

▷ **Factory productivity:** +40%

▷ **Education:** +20%

▷ **Bank and shop building cost:** -25%

▷ **Respect of all women:** -10%

SCENARIO STRATEGY

The scenario starts with three farms, a construction office, one dock, and a palace.

Build your tobacco farms around the dormant volcano, a little further from your existing infrastructure. Don't waste any time!

Your tobacco farms will be scattered all over the place. Make sure you build the cigar plants between the farms and the docks. You'll definitely need more than one dock in this scenario.

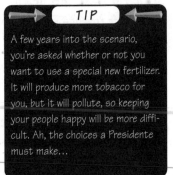

Take careful note of where tobacco will grow before you build any farms.

Because your victory goals are achieved as soon as you make your money, it's not as important to keep everything balanced. It must be just balanced enough to keep you in power. Get four cigar factories going as soon as possible, and don't overlook the factory upgrades.

> **TIP**
>
> A few years into the scenario, you're asked whether or not you want to use a special new fertilizer. It will produce more tobacco for you, but it will pollute, so keeping your people happy will be more difficult. Ah, the choices a Presidente must make...

APPENDIX A: CHEAT CODES

> "The fact is that a man who wants to act virtuously in every way necessarily comes to grief among so many who are not virtuous."
>
> —Machiavelli

Are the people revolting more than usual? Did that great economic plan not work out? Relax, el Presidente. You are truly gifted and can alter even the whims of fate.

MORE MONEY

Short on cash? Press and hold the Control key and type in **pesos**. This boosts your treasury by 20 grand. You can type this as often as you like, although your treasury may burst—I do not know, el Presidente.

Since a lot of the challenge of Tropico comes from trying to get the island running on very little capital, I advise using this cheat only in dire emergencies, but your Excellency, the island is yours to rule as you see fit.

HAPPY CITIZENS

Ah, the people are protesting or decrying your policies, and you just need them happy a little longer. Press and hold the Control key and type in **contento**. This improves their happiness by 10%. Keep in mind, however, that this is only a temporary fix.

You can always enter the cheat a second or third time, but a better strategy would be to find a way to keep your people happy by providing them with the things they desire.

APPENDIX B: BUILDINGS & STRUCTURES QUICK REFERENCE

"A revolution is an opinion which has found its bayonets."

—Napoleon

Your Excellency, for your convenience, this appendix lists all the buildings and structures that you might care to build during your tenure. May it aid your already gifted decision-making prowess. Viva el presidente!

INFRASTRUCTURE

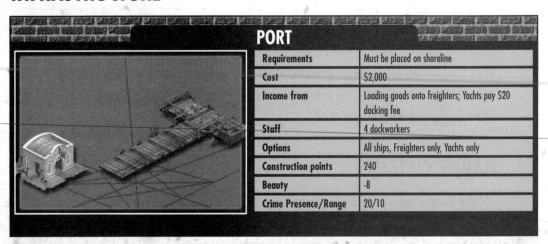

PORT

Requirements	Must be placed on shoreline
Cost	$2,000
Income from	Loading goods onto freighters; Yachts pay $20 docking fee
Staff	4 dockworkers
Options	All ships, Freighters only, Yachts only
Construction points	240
Beauty	-8
Crime Presence/Range	20/10

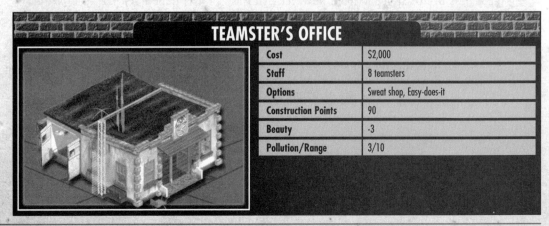

TEAMSTER'S OFFICE

Cost	$2,000
Staff	8 teamsters
Options	Sweat shop, Easy-does-it
Construction Points	90
Beauty	-3
Pollution/Range	3/10

AIRPORT

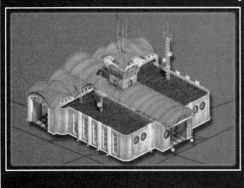

Cost	$16,000
Income From	$100 for coach tickets, $200 for first-class tickets
Staff	2 engineers (college educated)
Upgrades	*Enhanced terminal*: $6,000 (2 planes can use the airport at once)
	Control tower: $8,000 + 10 Mw electricity (larger planes, with up to 2/3 more passengers, can land at the airport)
Options	Coach service, first-class service
Construction Points	1000
Beauty	-8

CONSTRUCTION OFFICE

Cost	$1,000
Staff	8 laborers
Options	Sweat shop, Easy-does-it
Construction Points	60
Beauty	-2
Pollution/Range	3/10

ELECTRIC POWER PLANT

Cost	$17,000
Staff	6 engineers (college educated)
Options	Coal, Gas
Construction Points	300
Beauty	-15
Crime Presence/Range	5/10
Pollution/Range	30/15

ELECTRIC SUBSTATION

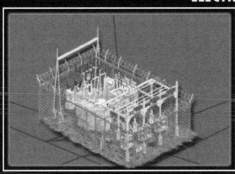

Requirements	Electric Power Plant
Cost	$2,000
Construction Points	60
Beauty	-3
Pollution/Range	5/10

BANK

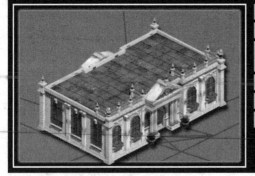

Cost	$8,000
Staff	5 bankers (college educated)
Options	Urban development, Presidential slush fund, Tourist's offshore banking
Construction Points	150
Beauty	-3
Police Presence/Range	8/10

HOUSING

SHACK

Cost	N/A
Income From	N/A
Houses	1 family
Base Housing Quality	5
Notes	Can be bulldozed
Beauty	-2
Crime Presence/Range	5/10

BUNKHOUSE

Cost	$350
Income From	Rent
Houses	2 families
Base Housing Quality	25
Options	Normal Maintenance, Roach Patrol
Construction Points	30

TENEMENT

Cost	$4,500
Income From	Rent
Houses	12 families
Base Housing Quality	35
Options	Normal Maintenance, Roach Patrol
Construction Points	300
Beauty	-5
Crime Presence/Range	12/10

COUNTRY HOUSE

Cost	$500
Income From	Rent
Houses	1 family
Base Housing Quality	50
Notes	Two styles of house
Construction Points	40

APARTMENT

Cost	$5,000
Income From	Rent
Houses	6 families
Base Housing Quality	60
Options	Normal Maintenance, Roach Patrol
Construction Points	230
Beauty	-2
Crime Presence/Range	3/10

HOUSE

Cost	$1,000
Income From	Rent
Houses	1 family
Base Housing Quality	70
Notes	3 styles of house
Construction Points	50

LUXURY HOUSE

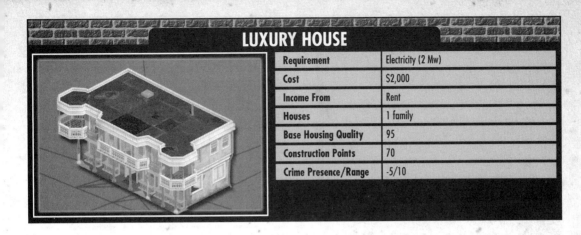

Requirement	Electricity (2 Mw)
Cost	$2,000
Income From	Rent
Houses	1 family
Base Housing Quality	95
Construction Points	70
Crime Presence/Range	-5/10

SIMPLE INDUSTRY

RANCH

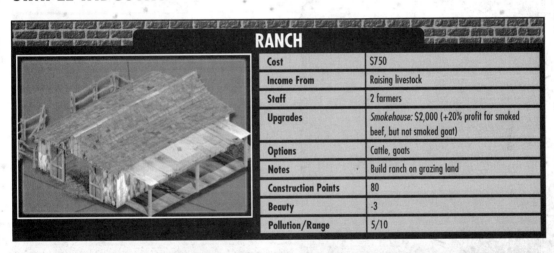

Cost	$750
Income From	Raising livestock
Staff	2 farmers
Upgrades	*Smokehouse:* $2,000 (+20% profit for smoked beef, but not smoked goat)
Options	Cattle, goats
Notes	Build ranch on grazing land
Construction Points	80
Beauty	-3
Pollution/Range	5/10

FARM

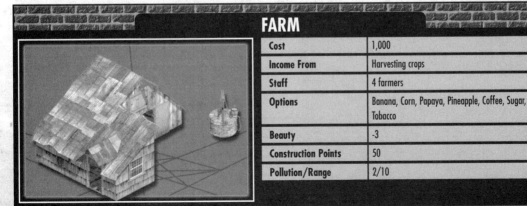

Cost	1,000
Income From	Harvesting crops
Staff	4 farmers
Options	Banana, Corn, Papaya, Pineapple, Coffee, Sugar, Tobacco
Beauty	-3
Construction Points	50
Pollution/Range	2/10

LOGGING CAMP

Cost	$1,500
Income From	Cutting down trees
Staff	8 lumberjacks
Upgrades	*Tool shop:* $3,000 (-40% cutting time) *Horticulture station:* $1,500 (double-speed tree regrowth)
Options	Clear cut, Selective harvest
Construction Points	110
Beauty	-10
Crime Presence/Range	5/10
Pollution/Range	10/10

FISHERMAN'S WHARF

Requirements	Must be on the shore
Cost	$3,000
Income From	Fishing
Staff	4 fishermen
Options	Clean waste disposal, Back to the sea
Notes	4 facings for wharf
Construction Points	90
Beauty	-5
Crime Presence/Range	5/10
Pollution/Range	15/15

MINE

Cost	$3,000
Income From	Mining
Staff	8 miners
Upgrades	*Crusher:* $1,500 + 5 Mw electricity (+30% bauxite per load, +15% iron per load) *Screener:* $3,000 + 10 Mw electricity (+20% gold per load, +10% other minerals) *Separator:* $5,000 + 10 Mw electricity (+40% iron per load)
Options	Bauxite, Gold, Iron, all metals
Construction Points	90
Beauty	-15
Crime Presence/Range	5/10
Pollution/Range	15/10

INDUSTRIAL STRUCTURES

LUMBER MILL

Requirements	Logging Camp
Cost	$5,000
Income From	Converting trees to lumber
Staff	5 workers with high school education
Upgrades	*Sawdust burner:* $2,000 (-50% pollution) *Power saw:* $2,000 + 10 mw electricity (+30% worker production) *Log Debarker:* $3,000 + 5 mw electricity (+25 % worker production, but 10% more logs required)
Options	Sweat Shop, Easy-Does-It
Construction Points	240
Beauty	-12
Crime Presence/Range	5/10
Pollution/Range	30/20

CIGAR FACTORY

Requirements	Tobacco farm
Cost	$10,000
Income From	Cigar manufacture
Staff	8 workers with high school education
Upgrades	*Skylights:* $5,000 (+ 15% worker satisfaction) *Climate Control:* $6,000 +5 Mw electricity (-20% raw materials per cigar) *Auto-roller:* $12,000 + 10 Mw electricity (+50% worker production, -10% value each cigar [hand-rolled cigars are worth more per cigar])
Options	Sweat Shop, Easy-Does It
Construction Points	300
Beauty	-10
Crime Presence/Range	5/10
Pollution/Range	5/15

JEWELRY FACTORY

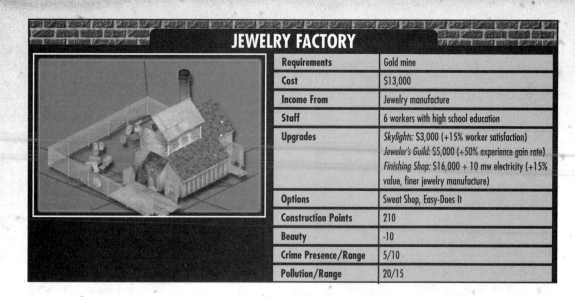

Requirements	Gold mine
Cost	$13,000
Income From	Jewelry manufacture
Staff	6 workers with high school education
Upgrades	*Skylights:* $3,000 (+15% worker satisfaction) *Jeweler's Guild:* $5,000 (+50% experience gain rate) *Finishing Shop:* $16,000 + 10 mw electricity (+15% value, finer jewelry manufacture)
Options	Sweat Shop, Easy-Does It
Construction Points	210
Beauty	-10
Crime Presence/Range	5/10
Pollution/Range	20/15

CANNERY

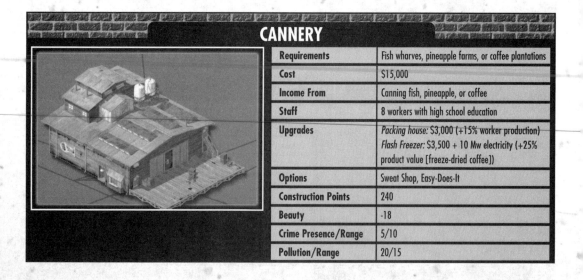

Requirements	Fish wharves, pineapple farms, or coffee plantations
Cost	$15,000
Income From	Canning fish, pineapple, or coffee
Staff	8 workers with high school education
Upgrades	*Packing house:* $3,000 (+15% worker production) *Flash Freezer:* $3,500 + 10 Mw electricity (+25% product value [freeze-dried coffee])
Options	Sweat Shop, Easy-Does-It
Construction Points	240
Beauty	-18
Crime Presence/Range	5/10
Pollution/Range	20/15

RUM DISTILLERY

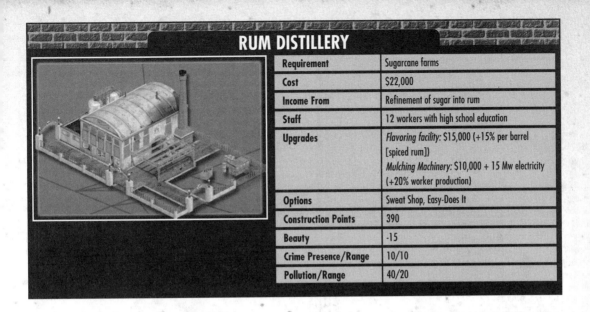

Requirement	Sugarcane farms
Cost	$22,000
Income From	Refinement of sugar into rum
Staff	12 workers with high school education
Upgrades	*Flavoring facility:* $15,000 (+15% per barrel [spiced rum]) *Mulching Machinery:* $10,000 + 15 Mw electricity (+20% worker production)
Options	Sweat Shop, Easy-Does It
Construction Points	390
Beauty	-15
Crime Presence/Range	10/10
Pollution/Range	40/20

ENTERTAINMENT

PUB

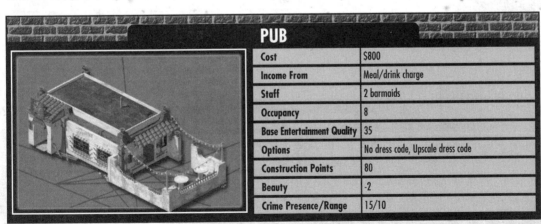

Cost	$800
Income From	Meal/drink charge
Staff	2 barmaids
Occupancy	8
Base Entertainment Quality	35
Options	No dress code, Upscale dress code
Construction Points	80
Beauty	-2
Crime Presence/Range	15/10

RESTAURANT

Cost	$2,000
Income From	Meal charge
Staff	2 cooks
Occupancy	10
Base Entertainment Quality	40
Options	Paper placements, Cloth napkins, Linen tablecloths
Construction Points	130
Beauty	-3
Crime Presence/Range	4/10

NIGHTCLUB

Requirements	Pub, 8 Mw electricity
Cost	$4,000
Income From	Admission fee
Staff	4 barmaids
Occupancy	15
Base Entertainment Quality	70
Options	No dress code, Upscale dress code
Construction Points	250
Beauty	-2
Crime Presence/Range	20/10

GOURMET RESTAURANT

Requirements	Restaurant, 5 Mw electricity
Cost	$3,000
Income From	Meal charge
Staff	4 cooks
Occupancy	12
Base Entertainment Quality	80
Options	Paper placemats, Cloth napkins, Linen tablecloths
Beauty	-2
Construction Points	160
Crime Presence/Range	2/10

SPORTS COMPLEX

Requirements	20 Mw electricity
Cost	$25,000
Income From	Admission fee
Staff	6 athletes with high school education
Occupancy	24
Base entertainment Quality	60
Options	*No booze allowed:* Just what it says. *Let it flow:* Scares off non-drinkers, revenue +$3 per customer
Construction Points	570
Beauty	-10
Crime Presence/Range	10/10

CASINO

Requirements	25 Mw electricity
Cost	$10,000
Income From	Admission fee
Staff	4 pit bosses with high school education
Occupancy	24
Base Entertainment Quality	55
Options	Nickel slot machines, Black jack, Baccarat
Construction Points	240
Beauty	-5
Crime Presence/Range	15/10

CABARET

Cost	$4,000
Income From	Admission fee
Staff	3 showgirls
Occupancy	9
Base Entertainment Quality	60
Options	No dress code, Upscale dress code
Construction Points	150
Beauty	-8
Crime Presence/Range	15/10

TOURISM

CHEAP HOTEL

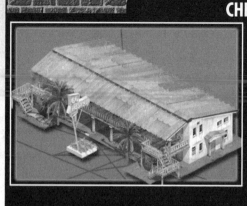

Cost	$3,000
Income From	Nightly rate
Staff	2 maids
Occupancy	10 couples
Base Tourism Quality	30
Tourism Rating of Area	Low-class
Options	Auto-fee (50-100% occupancy), Manual
Construction Points	140
Beauty	-10
Pollution/Range	2/10
Crime Presence/Range	10/10

BUNGALOW

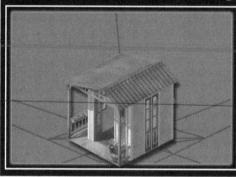

Cost	$400
Income From	Nightly rate
Staff	1 maid
Occupancy	1 couple
Base Tourism Quality	60
Tourism Rating of Area	Middle-class
Options	Auto-fee (50-100% occupancy), Manual
Construction Points	10

HOTEL

Cost	$5,000
Income From	Nightly rate
Staff	3 maids
Occupancy	12 couples
Base Tourism Quality	50
Tourism Rating of Area	Middle-class
Options	Auto-fee (50-100% occupancy), Manual
Construction Points	180
Pollution/Range	3/10
Crime Presence/Range	5/10

LUXURY HOTEL

Requirements	15 Mw electricity
Cost	$10,000
Income From	Nightly rate
Staff	6 maids
Occupancy	15 couples
Base Tourism Quality	80
Tourism Rating of Area	High-class
Options	Auto-fee (50-100% occupancy), Manual
Construction Points	320
Pollution/Range	4/10
Crime Presence/Range	5/10

BEACH SITE

Requirements	Any hotel
Cost	$500
Income From	Admission fee
Staff	1 attendant
Occupancy	10
Base Entertainment Quality	50
Options	No dress code, Upscale dress code
Construction Points	40
Beauty	5

SCENIC OUTLOOK

Requirements	Any hotel
Cost	$1,000
Income From	Admission fee
Staff	1 attendant
Occupancy	6
Base Entertainment Quality	50
Options	Mimeographed handout, 4-color brochure
Notes	Environmental quality very strong
Construction Points	40

SOUVENIR SHOP

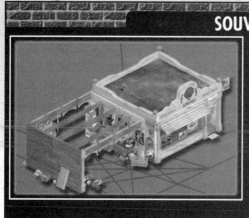

Requirements	Any hotel
Cost	$1,250
Income From	Tourist purchases
Staff	2 shopkeepers with high school education
Occupancy	10
Base Entertainment Quality	35
Options	T-shirts, arts and crafts
Construction Points	80
Beauty	-2
Crime Presence/Range	2/10

ARCHEOLOGICAL SITE

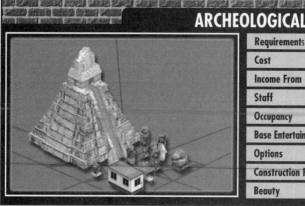

Requirements	Ancient ruin
Cost	$2,000
Income From	Admission fee
Staff	2 professors (college educated)
Occupancy	10
Base Entertainment Quality	70
Options	Mimeographed handout, 4-color brochure
Construction Points	40
Beauty	12

POOL

Requirements	Any hotel
Cost	$4,000
Income From	Admission fee
Staff	2 attendants
Occupancy	16
Base Entertainment Quality	60
Options	No dress code, Upscale dress code
Construction Points	50
Crime Presence/Range	2/10

SPA

Requirements	Any hotel
Cost	$5,000
Income From	Admission fee
Staff	3 attendants
Occupancy	9
Base Entertainment Quality	90
Options	No dress code, Upscale dress code
Construction Points	80
Crime Presence/Range	2/10

GOVERNMENT

PALACE

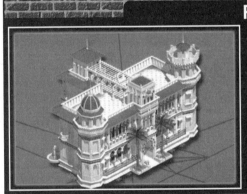

Staff	4 soldiers
Options	Normal training, Special op training
Construction Points	500
Beauty	5
Police Presence/Range	20/15

DIPLOMATIC MINISTRY

Requirements	Electric power plant
Cost	$5,000
Staff	4 bureaucrats (high school education)
Options	Neutral policy, Pro-American, Pro-Russian
Construction Points	200

POLICE STATION

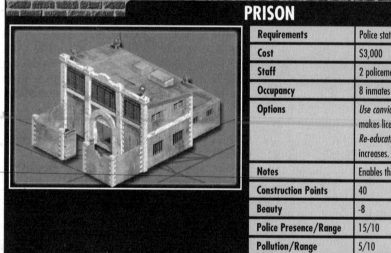

Cost	$2,000
Staff	6 policemen (high school education)
Options	Normal training, Special op training
Construction Points	90
Beauty	-2
Police Presence/Range	18/15

PRISON

Requirements	Police station
Cost	$3,000
Staff	2 policemen
Occupancy	8 inmates
Options	*Use convict labor:* Each month, every prisoner makes license plates worth $5 *Re-education:* Prisoner's respect for regime increases. Maybe.
Notes	Enables the Arrest edict
Construction Points	40
Beauty	-8
Police Presence/Range	15/10
Pollution/Range	5/10

GUARD STATION

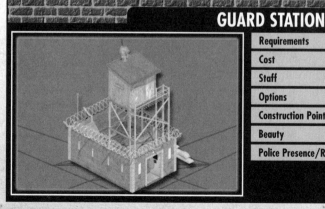

Requirements	At least one working general per guard station
Cost	$1,500
Staff	3 soldiers
Options	Normal training, Special op training
Construction Points	50
Beauty	-5
Police Presence/Range	10/10

ARMORY

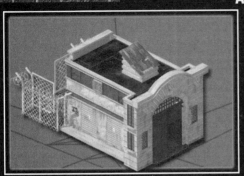

Cost	$3,000
Staff	3 generals (college education)
Options	Normal training, Special op training
Construction Points	150
Beauty	-3

IMMIGRATION OFFICE

Cost	$2,500
Staff	3 bureaucrats (high school education)
Options	Open door immigration, Skilled workers welcome, Tropico first, Love it or leave it, Nobody gets out of here alive
Notes	Only 1 per island
Construction Points	800
Beauty	-2

RADIO STATION

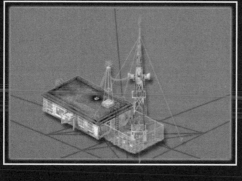

Requirements	10 Mw electricity
Cost	$10,000
Staff	2 journalists (college education)
Options	*El Presidente:* Air your musings 24 hours, which increases the respect the people feel for you *Radio free Tropico:* Gives a plus to liberty to all within range. *Menudo's greatest hits:* Foreign broadcaster will pay you so much a month to play music aimed at 4-25 year old Tropicans *Baja Bachata:* Foreign broadcaster will pay you so much a month to play the music of the common people. *Ossified Opera:* Foreign broadcaster will pay you so much a month to play music beloved by the educated set.
Notes	Only 4 radio stations allowed per island.
Construction Points	160
Beauty	-10
Crime Presence/Range	5/10

NEWSPAPER

Cost	$7,500
Staff	4 journalists (college education)
Options	*Voice of the workers:* +1 to +10 percent with communist faction, depending on experience of journalists. *Financial times:* +1 to +10 % with capitalists. *Soldado de fortuna:* +1 to 10% with militants. *The word of God:* +1 to 10% with religious faction. *Coupons 'n' more:* Foreign publisher will pay you so much a month per adult Tropican to print their coupons, again partly dependent on journalist experience.
Notes	4 allowed per island
Construction Points	240
Beauty	-10
Pollution/Range	5/10
Crime Presence/Range	5/10

TV STATION

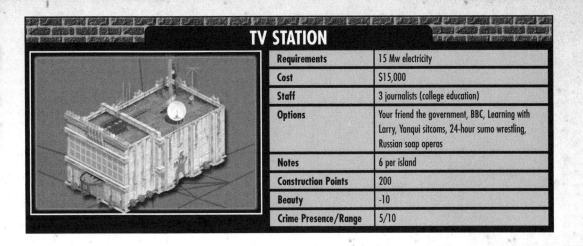

Requirements	15 Mw electricity
Cost	$15,000
Staff	3 journalists (college education)
Options	Your friend the government, BBC, Learning with Larry, Yanqui sitcoms, 24-hour sumo wrestling, Russian soap operas
Notes	6 per island
Construction Points	200
Beauty	-10
Crime Presence/Range	5/10

HUMAN SERVICES

CLINIC

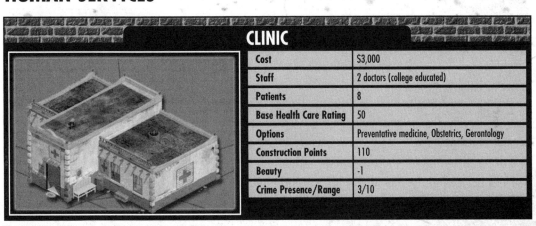

Cost	$3,000
Staff	2 doctors (college educated)
Patients	8
Base Health Care Rating	50
Options	Preventative medicine, Obstetrics, Gerontology
Construction Points	110
Beauty	-1
Crime Presence/Range	3/10

HOSPITAL

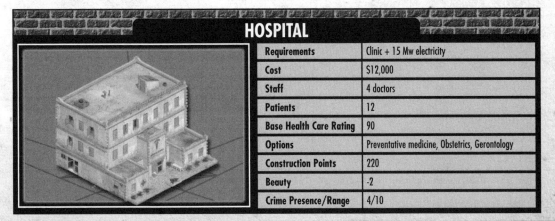

Requirements	Clinic + 15 Mw electricity
Cost	$12,000
Staff	4 doctors
Patients	12
Base Health Care Rating	90
Options	Preventative medicine, Obstetrics, Gerontology
Construction Points	220
Beauty	-2
Crime Presence/Range	4/10

CHURCH

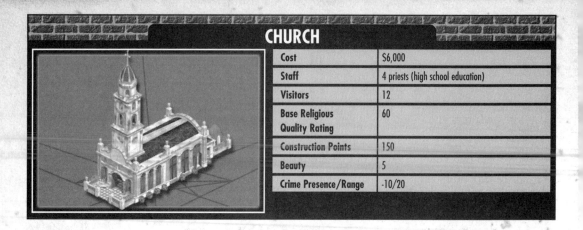

Cost	$6,000
Staff	4 priests (high school education)
Visitors	12
Base Religious Quality Rating	60
Construction Points	150
Beauty	5
Crime Presence/Range	-10/20

CATHEDRAL

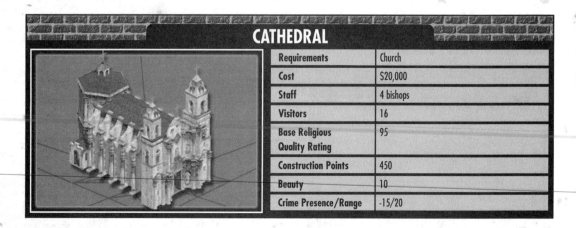

Requirements	Church
Cost	$20,000
Staff	4 bishops
Visitors	16
Base Religious Quality Rating	95
Construction Points	450
Beauty	10
Crime Presence/Range	-15/20

HIGH SCHOOL

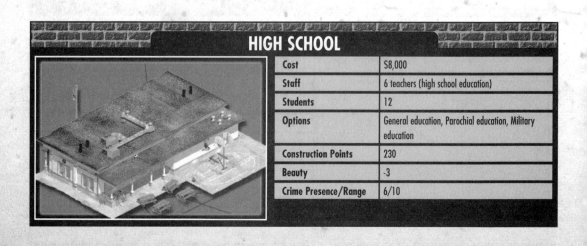

Cost	$8,000
Staff	6 teachers (high school education)
Students	12
Options	General education, Parochial education, Military education
Construction Points	230
Beauty	-3
Crime Presence/Range	6/10

COLLEGE

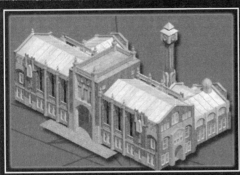

Requirements	High school
Cost	$12,000
Staff	8 professors (college educated)
Students	16
Options	General education, Parochial education, Military education
Construction Points	340
Beauty	5
Crime Presence/Range	4/10

MARKETPLACE

Cost	$500
Income From	Food purchase
Staff	1 shopkeeper (high school educated)
Construction Points	30
Crime Presence/Range	4/10

APPENDIX C: BUILDING & OCCUPATION QUICK REFERENCE

> "Politics divides us, but humanity unites us."
>
> —Castro

El Presidente, if you need a quick refresher course on qualifications needed for a particular place of employment, please make use of this. I'm not saying that you're not intelligent, el supremo, but use it at your discretion.

Building/Structure	Education Requirement
Beach site	Uneducated
Pool	Uneducated
Scenic outlook	Uneducated
Spa	Uneducated
Nightclub	Uneducated
Pub	Uneducated
Gourmet Restaurant	Uneducated
Restaurant	Uneducated
Dock	Uneducated
Farm	Uneducated
Ranch	Uneducated
Fisherman's wharf	Uneducated
Construction office	Uneducated
Logging camp	Uneducated
Bungalow	Uneducated
Cheap motel	Uneducated
Hotel	Uneducated
Luxury hotel	Uneducated
Mine	Uneducated
Cabaret	Uneducated
Teamster's office	Uneducated

Building/Structure	Education Requirement
Sports complex	High School
Immigration office	High School
Diplomatic ministry	High School
Cannery	High School
Cigar factory	High School
Jewelry factory	High School
Lumber mill	High School
Rum distillery	High School
Casino	High School
Police office	High School
Prison	High School
Church	High School
Marketplace	High School
Souvenir shop	High School
Palace	High School
Guard post	High School
High School (teacher)	High School

Building/Structure	Education Requirement
Bank	College
Cathedral	College
Clinic	College
Hospital	College
Airport	College
Electric power plant	College
Armory	College
Newspaper	College
Radio station	College
TV station	College
Archeological site	College
University	College

Since you are so busy with your daily duties, el supremo, we thought it would be generous to include a listing of each type of person on the island and their occupation of choice. Please use it as you see fit, your Excellency.

Uneducated

Job	Places Worked
Attendant	Beach site, Pool, Scenic outlook, Spa
Barmaid	Nightclub, Pub
Cook	Gourmet Restaurant, Restaurant
Dockworker	Dock
Farmer	Farm, Ranch
Fisherman	Fisherman's wharf
Laborer	Construction office
Lumberjack	Logging camp
Maid	Bungalow, Cheap motel, Hotel, Luxury hotel
Miner	Mine
Showgirl	Cabaret
Teamster	Teamster's office

High School Educated

Job	Places Worked
Athlete	Sports complex
Bureaucrat	Immigration office, Diplomatic ministry
Factory Worker	Cannery, Cigar factory, Jewelry factory, Lumber mill, Rum distillery
Pit Boss	Casino
Policeman	Police office, Prison
Priest	Church
Shopkeeper	Market, Souvenir shop
Soldier	Palace, Guard post
Teacher	High school

College Educated

Job	Places Worked
Banker	Bank
Bishop	Cathedral
Doctor	Clinic, Hospital
Engineer	Airport, electric power plant
General	Armory
Journalist	Newspaper, Radio station, TV station
Professor	Archeological site, University

Other People

Job	Places Worked
Students	Attend schools to learn more skills
Mothers	Return to the workforce when youngest child reaches the age of 8
Children	Attempt to find work at age 13
Retirees	Wander the island
Rebels	Hide in the jungles, waiting to ambush your island

INDEX

empathatic ruler, 31
empty spaces in buildings, 81
entertainment, 47–48, 104–107, 173–175
entrepreneurial ruler, 32
environment, 50–54
environmentalists, 54

F

factions, 54–55
family values, ruler, 25
farmer ruler, 15
farms, 62–64, 99, 169
financial genius ruler, 29
finishing shop, jewelry factory, 70
fisherman's wharf, industry and, 64, 100, 170
flash freezer, cannery, 70
flatulent ruler, 36
flavoring facility, rum distillery, 70
flaws, ruler, 33–41
foreign policy, 56–57
        edicts, 124, 127–128
fortunate son, ruler, 17
Free Elections special circumstance, 10
Fruitas scenario, 152–153

G

generalissimo, ruler, 19
gold mines, 66
gourmet restaurants, entertainment and, 106, 174
government, 68–69, 113–118, 179–181
great schmoozola ruler, 41
green thumb ruler, 30
guard station, government, 115, 180

H

hardworking ruler, 29
Harvard U., ruler, 14
headliner, economic policy edicts, 131
health care, 48–49
heir apparent, ruler, 28
heretics, people edicts, 126
high-class tourists, 72
high-school educated workers, 83–84
high schools, human services, 121, 183
hospitals, human services, 119, 183
hotels, tourism and, 109, 176
housing, 45–46, 94–97, 97, 167–169, 168
human services, 119–122, 183–185

I

immigrants, 10
Immigrants Out! special circumstance, 10
immigration office, government, 116, 181

incorruptible ruler, 32
industrial structures, 171–173
industry, 66–71, 98–100, 169–170
        structures, 101–103
industry ad campaign, economic policy edicts, 130
infrastructure, 68–69
        buildings and, 90–93
inquisitions, political/religious edicts, 135
intimidation, factions and, 54
invasion, foreign policy and, 57
iron mines, 66
Isle De Foresta scenario, 154–155

J-K

jails, political/religious edict, 136
Jeweler's Guild, jewelry factory, 70
jewelry factory, industry and, 70, 102, 172
job skills, 79

KGB installed ruler, 26
kleptomaniac ruler, 34

L

landscaping, 123
leftist author, ruler, 17
literacy program, social edicts, 139
log debarker, lumber mill, 69
logging camp, industry and, 99, 170
logging camps, industry and, 65
Los Exconvictos scenario, 154–156
low-class tourists, 72
lumber mill, industry and, 69, 101, 171
luxury homes, housing, 97, 169
luxury hotels, tourism and, 109, 177

M

man of the people, ruler, 16
Mardi Gras, economic policy edicts, 133
marketplace, human services, 185
martial law, political/religious edicts, 136
Mi Corazon scenario, 156–158
middle-class tourists, 72
militarists, 54
military coup, ruler, 25
minerals, 9
miners, ruler, 14
mines, industry and, 65–66, 100, 170
money, 10
        cheat codes, 163
moronic ruler, 38
Moscow U., ruler, 13
Mother of All Cigars scenario, 161–162
mulching machinery, rum distillery, 70